STARTING TODAY 100 POEMS FOR OBAMA'S FIRST 100 DAYS

STARTING

TODAY100

POEMS FOR

OBAMA'S

FIRST 100

DAYS

Edited by **Rachel Zucker** &

Arielle Greenberg

University of Iowa Press IOWA CITY

University of Iowa Press, Iowa City 52242

Copyright © 2010 by the University of Iowa Press

www.uiowapress.org

Printed in the United States of America

Design by Richard Hendel

The University of Iowa Press, a member of Green Press
Initiative, is committed to preserving natural resources.

Printed on acid-free paper

Library of Congress Cataloging-in-Publication Data

Starting today: 100 poems for Obama's first 100 days /
edited by Rachel Zucker and Arielle Greenberg.

p.   cm.

Includes index.

ISBN-13: 978-1-58729-871-4 (pbk.)

ISBN-10: 1-58729-871-6 (pbk.)

1. Obama, Barack—Poetry.   2. Presidents—United
States—Poetry.   3. United States—Politics and
government—2009—Poetry.   4. Political poetry,
American.   I. Zucker, Rachel.   II. Greenberg, Arielle.

PS595.O23S73 2010   2009031225

811'.608035873932—dc22

Starting today, we must pick ourselves up, dust ourselves off, and begin
again the work of remaking America.
—President Barack Obama, January 20, 2009

Poetry is a response to the daily necessity of getting the world right.
—Wallace Stevens

you were the one today I wanted to talk to
you were someone I could be happy
losing at last myself in singing with
no longer everyone and I   *but* we
—Craig Arnold

Contents

Foreword

RITA DOVE

Poetry is alive and well. Sounds pat, I know—but it is, sadly, not such a foregone conclusion. I was lucky enough to have been poet laureate during the golden years of the Clinton administration, when poetry, among other arts, was acknowledged as an important and integral part of American culture. Then came the cultural wasteland and political nightmare of Bush-Cheney . . . not that W's White House, at least in the early years, didn't try to use poetry as a fig leaf. I became quickly aware of the size and protective coloration of that leaf. In the early months of the right-wing power-grab, a high-ranking moderate Republican whom I knew to be a decent man suggested me for a seat on the National Council on the Arts. When a smooth-voiced Bush drone phoned to conduct initial interviews for the honorary post (a presidential nomination that requires Senate approval), the customary inquiries became increasingly tainted with political innuendo until she asked me if I had "voted for the president." The moment I informed her that such a question was inappropriate under the rules of vetting procedure, my candidacy died. Still, the notion seemed to persist that a former poet laureate who counted a few moderate conservatives among her personal friends might be useful. I politely declined a dinner invitation to the White House a few days before 9/11, and when, during the fraudulent WMD frenzy leading up to the Iraq war, Laura Bush tried to organize a poetry evening at 1600 Pennsylvania Avenue, I chose simply not to respond to the invitation; only after Sam Hamill's brilliant public declaration that he would accept in order to read antiwar poetry for the occasion did the media come calling, and I could tell them what I thought of the "officials" running our country.

"Poets," Shelley declared, "are the unacknowledged legislators of the world." How can this be? In his *Defence of Poetry* (written in response to Thomas Peacock's assertion that poetry bears little relevance in an age of science and technology—sound familiar?), Shelley asserted that poetry "awakens and enlarges the mind itself by rendering it the receptacle of a thousand unapprehended combinations of thought," because it is "a sword of lightning, ever unsheathed, which consumes the scabbard that would contain it." No wonder one of the first objectives in a military coup is to gain control of the media. No wonder writers—and poets, especially poets—are jailed by dictators all over the world. No wonder the surge of unprecedented hope in this country, sprung from the unwelcoming gray scarp of nearly a decade of palaver, makes us feel tentative, yet exuberantly alive.

The first one hundred days of a new era: one hundred breaths of fresh air after nearly three thousand days of staleness. One hundred days and counting. And though a hundred days are nothing like a decade and nowhere near a century, the world can change in a few months, in a few days, in an instant. Suddenly, there's a frisson in the air—risible, catching—and to our amazement turning into a new reality. Since November 2008, passersby do their passing with eyes sparkling, a smile tugging at the cautionary mask. Can you see it? A twitch. A twinkle. Clustered strangers and spontaneous smiles, short bursts of laughter. Spirits lifted even as the markets crash. Black girls playing in front of a white house. Bare arms on women over forty. A little black dog with a little black name, a blues man's moniker.

It's as if we have shaken off a troubled sleep, still a little dazed but relieved to find all toes and fingers accounted for. It's as if America the Beautiful has struck up a conversation with herself, eager for the news which William Carlos Williams said could not be found in newspapers but without which we perish bit by bit every day. Can you hear it, the expectant murmur breaking through the background roar—echoing over the high seas and on dry ground, from ivy-walled campuses and brick tenements, down asphalted boulevards and rutted tractor lanes?

And who better to chronicle such Change but our poets—to distill into words the thrilling murmur that keeps breaking through the background roar? Here in these pages, bearing witness to the first hundred days of the Obama administration, we have the confident and diverse voices of those Shelley called "the unacknowledged legislators": our poets, America's cantors—singing, as Stevie Wonder says, in the *Key of Life*.

Introduction

RACHEL ZUCKER AND ARIELLE GREENBERG

On the day before Barack Obama's inauguration we called each other, from the Upper West Side of Manhattan to small-town midcoast Maine, flushed with excitement and optimism about the new president, about a new era in which we might feel proud to be Americans, and our talk turned to ways we could commemorate and celebrate this moment through poetry. As poets, we were thrilled that our president-elect seemed to care deeply about language and that he had chosen Elizabeth Alexander—a serious and important poet—to read at his inauguration.

In those jittery, preinaugural hours, it became clear to us that our exhilaration stemmed, in part, from the knowledge that we were not alone in our enthusiasm. We knew others felt called to action just as we did. That same afternoon we compiled an e-mail list of poets—friends, acquaintances, and folks we admire—from across the country and across generations. Could we get ninety-nine poets to commit to writing a new poem during the first one hundred carefully watched days of the new presidency? And could we get them to respond overnight, so that our project would coincide with Barack Obama beginning his job? Yes, we could! Poets wrote back immediately, and with gusto.

By the time President Obama said, in his inaugural speech, "Starting today, we must pick ourselves up, dust ourselves off, and begin again the work of remaking America," we were ready. By the time Elizabeth Alexander said, tremulously, "In today's sharp sparkle, this winter air, / any thing can be made, any sentence begun," we were ready. Ninety-nine poets were ready to begin sentences, ready to write a poem that responded to the state of the nation and to share this poem with others.

This project has been very much a twenty-first-century one, and in its original incarnation as a blog it relied on twenty-first-century technology. Once we had all the poets lined up, we assigned each poet a day on which to write his or her poem. We asked the poets to write their poems no more than one day before, or better yet, *on* the assigned day. We didn't want one hundred inaugural poems. We wanted poems that reflected the latest news, the changing season, the evolving zeitgeist. In this sense these hundred poems are a kind of reportage.

In the first hundred days, quite a bit happened. President Obama took the oath of office (twice); appointed dozens of aides (a few of whom hadn't paid all their taxes); signed a stimulus bill and a fair pay act; proposed a budget; set a new stem cell policy; released torture memos and announced he would close Guantánamo; hosted a seder; opened a door to Cuba; bailed out GM and Chrysler; proposed mortgage relief; called AIG's bonuses an outrage; met cheering supporters and glad-handing pols in Ottawa, London, Strasbourg, Prague, Istanbul, Baghdad, and Mexico City (not to mention Elkhart, Indiana; Fort Myers, Florida; Chicago, Illinois; Williamsburg, Virginia; Mesa, Arizona; and Cherry Point, North Carolina); bought a dog; negotiated with pirates; and told stories at the Easter Egg Roll. Meanwhile, the North Koreans fired a rocket into the ocean; same-sex marriage made headway in Iowa and Vermont; and the market was dragged down further under its own downward momentum.

The poets in this collection write about much of this news — and about stories and moments the media didn't cover. The poets write about their children, their parents, about windshield washers, garlic toast, physical ailments, outer space, death, bras, the weather, flowers, getting blood drawn, and basketball, just to name a few.

Another event happened during these hundred days that became terribly, necessarily public: we were shocked and worried when Craig Arnold, a wonderful poet and one of our contributors and friends, went missing on April 27 while researching volcanoes in Japan. His family and friends rallied — contacting the media and government officials — to encourage the search for him to continue beyond the standard three-day period. We were heartbroken when, after more than ten days, Craig was not found. We feel honored that Craig is part of this project.

★

Many readers of this project have been interested in the process behind the writing of these poems, and we can report that many of the contributing poets (including ourselves) felt some healthy anxiety at the challenge of writing an occasional, political poem, a poem that would be almost instantly published without the luxury of multiple drafts and time for reflection. (For more on individual poets' processes, see the biographies section at the back of this book.) Of course, the spontaneity required was also part of the pleasure — these poems feel more urgent and have attracted a wider audience than poetry often does. The project illustrates how public, accessible, relevant, collaborative, and *democratic* poetry can be.

There is no one unifying theme or message in these poems, which is all to the good, but if we were to pick out a common thread, we think it would echo our president's message of personal responsibility, of loving this country enough to expect a great deal of it, and of having the courage to be hopeful. History will be the eventual judge of our hopefulness and of whether the sustained attention of these one hundred poems represents the beginning of a new epoch, but the fact of these poems, the eager throng of them—varied as they are in form, style, tone and intention—cannot be mistaken. We are proud and privileged to live at a time when poetry feels vital and alive.

ELIZABETH ALEXANDER

Praise Song for the Day

day

Each day we go about our business,
walking past each other, catching each other's
eyes or not, about to speak or speaking.

All about us is noise. All about us is
noise and bramble, thorn and din, each
one of our ancestors on our tongues.

Someone is stitching up a hem, darning
a hole in a uniform, patching a tire,
repairing the things in need of repair.

Someone is trying to make music somewhere,
with a pair of wooden spoons on an oil drum,
with cello, boom box, harmonica, voice.

A woman and her son wait for the bus.
A farmer considers the changing sky.
A teacher says, *Take out your pencils. Begin.*

We encounter each other in words, words
spiny or smooth, whispered or declaimed,
words to consider, reconsider.

We cross dirt roads and highways that mark
the will of some one and then others, who said
I need to see what's on the other side.

I know there's something better down the road.
We need to find a place where we are safe.
We walk into that which we cannot yet see.

Say it plain: that many have died for this day.
Sing the names of the dead who brought us here,
who laid the train tracks, raised the bridges,

picked the cotton and the lettuce, built
brick by brick the glittering edifices
they would then keep clean and work inside of.

Praise song for struggle, praise song for the day.
Praise song for every hand-lettered sign,
the figuring-it-out at kitchen tables.

Some live by *love thy neighbor as thyself*,
others by *first do no harm* or *take no more
than you need*. What if the mightiest word is love?

Love beyond marital, filial, national,
love that casts a widening pool of light,
love with no need to preempt grievance.

In today's sharp sparkle, this winter air,
any thing can be made, any sentence begun.
On the brink, on the brim, on the cusp,

praise song for walking forward in that light.

Poem

day 2

On Tuesday at noon the
sun suddenly came out I
swear I said to my
daughter something was happening but
what and the stars don't
care about us who we
elect or when we listen to
the radio and hear it
say President Obama is going
to shut down the prison
the stars don't care they
are forever exploding hydrogen atoms
slowly depleting dying like us
to them if they thought
at all they'd think everything
we do is in prison
the president said we could
write poems again saying "president"
that people would have to
think about not just understand
like he said "science is
coming, people" to which my
son said "did he say
science?" I said "I know
it's hard to believe but
the new president said science"

His Springboard Resolve

For his firmness is most fog horn.
For he's darning our fraying hem with fine thread; for he's following a plan.
Be it a progression from detention to due process.
Be it a declaration of Middle East and market collapse mazes unmazed.
Be it settled.

From this day forward, a little less fetus, a lot more science.
From this day forward, more angles, more angels.

In with the fluent, out with the foibles.
In with the factual, out with the furrowed.
In with fine-tuning, out with the cudgels.

Today, the shimmery window of the immediate.

More from those who pray in a mosque, in a temple. Less from the
    evangelical.
More service, less fretting.
More figuring, less guessing.
More giving, less getting.
No bitching.

Coming to a theatre near you, an outrageous congruity.
Coming to that theatre, an unprecedented logic.
Coming soon, endpoints.
Soon to come, time frames.

The sun is rising over rising water, over the desert's drying, over the dead
    and the dying.
The sun is rising; let it inflame us.

Overwinter

day

We have been waiting out the winter
for eight years.   I don't pretend
to talk for you   or my neighbors—
but I have been given   permission
to speak   on behalf   of mollusks, insects,
and various wily birds.   This is the price
and the   pleasure   of a new president:
those who were hushed   now feel
like they can finally   chatter and natter—
flex wing   and leg freely.   The clutch
of snails on the fence post   near
my house can finally   unclench
retreat to   damp underboards
of   the tool shed.   And I have it
on good authority   at least one
spicebush   and three swallowtails
have promised   to arrive   a few weeks
earlier from their Southern   holiday.
Those who   overwintered have returned.
Those who fell asleep   are awake.
I myself risk it all: I climb to the top
of a blade   of grass   the aperture   of my wingshell
opens and closes   and opens again.

Imagine All the People

Imagine being unable to imagine
another side.

What would you be?

A hill so steep you'd throw your thoughts against it?

Segregated schools?
A decider who never had to fight?

Without advance imagination
the people perish.

Would you be a grandmother who keeps hands warm
no matter where they're from?

Or would you be a moth-like hat
on the head of a singer
lifting her higher and higher?

Would you be a newspaper soldier, easy to burn?
Would you choose to be something you can never change?

Or would you hold up your arms
during the metamorphosis?

YVETTE THOMAS

Missing Metaphor for Time

Our last winter was furious.
In the gray and yellow dawns we cowered
we covered our heads.

World buckled at the margins redrawn
and drawn close
we shook.

No fruit fell.

Hope is wind chimes
and wind.

Change is

Man, Roll the Window Down!

On a slushed side street in the Bronx, a determined hustler
attacks your smudged windshield with enterprise, sloshes
the pane with old water and rocks a feverish squeegee
before you can mouth the word *no*. Stunned at a sluggish
stoplight, you have no choice but to force a smile, nod idly
while he stretches the busy machine of his body across
your hood and whips the gritty wet round and around.
It's a second before you notice that his mouth is moving,
that although he leapt to his task without warning, he is
now attempting to converse as men do, to pass the time,
to shoot the shit. You avoid the mouth, choosing instead
to scan the dank street for anything. There is lots to see—
stands tiled with cheap neon skullcaps, shuttered houses
of praise, the fragrant entrance to Chicken, Ribs & Such,
a city-assed woman drilling her stilettos into concrete,
the butcher shop with price tags pinned to sick meat.
In other words, there is nothing to see. He's still draped
across your Corolla, wiping, squeaking dry and mouthing.
Damned insistent now, he thumps on your windshield
and the light has changed now and behind you drivers
toot elegant fuck yous. You scramble for your wallet
because damn it, that's right, hell, you gotta pay the guy
for the gray crisscross swiping that dims the chaos
just enough. But what's the message of that mouth,
he needs you to know something, inside the huge O
of his wild miming there's a collision of collapsed teeth
and you slide your window down to a symphony of horn
and mad street spittle, and your hustler's message,
what he had to get across before he let you pull away
from that street light, *Obama! Obama! Obama! Obama!*
he spurt screeches, his eyes fevered with whiskey
and damn-it-all, no verbs or adornment, just *Obama!*
as if his wiping little life is stuck on triumph, as if

that's all anybody needs to know this day and as he
leans in to roar his one-word stanza, damn the money,
you see that every single one of those teeth, tilted
and pushing for real estate in his mouth, every single
one of them is a gold like you've never seen before.

LYN LIFSHIN

Michelle's Citrine Dress

color of where
something growing
starts. Spring. Clean
and new. The place
where a stem jolts
up from what nourished
and fed it. I think of
tulips when I think of
that dress, what's
alive and sunny,
sparkling and nothing
like the yellow tulips
I sent for what I
knew could be a
dying friend's
dying day

SASHA STEENSEN

Wintry Weather and Job Slaughter

day

All our tales are tall:
one week after the inauguration,
the lost *n* in auger bores its hole in the frozen ground.

Daily life is holy bedeviling.
Who but a witness tree knew
the axe is an American native?

First thing today, I had my blood drawn.
In the distant waiting room,
we have to start by listening, the president says.
To what?
To what's been lost.

Octuplets born today—
that many more platelets to count,
that many more ears to open,
mouths to shut,
jobs to lose,
snows to shovel.

All emotion that matters
securely hidden
buried in a bed of heartsease,
fog and grown-over ferns
the terrific green,
still frozen,
still freezing

which doesn't mean hope
isn't eight times hotter
this time of year
just eight times
over
and melting
what?
fear?

My young saplings
and their hatchlings.

New Time Old Time

day **10**

The unchosen have always been the starbeams
for the poor, the tortured and beaten, the homeless,
the suffocated. They have been the wind that bursts
open poppies in an endless field, just as this morning
the January wind blew the seeds of this poem jotted
down with coffee 3 days before my daughter's 39th birthday.
She is, at this moment, in a classroom downtown studying
nursing, while her daughter, my little Izzie, sits
at Wanda's Daycare spilling blocks onto the carpet
with no awareness of the children's blood spilling
in Congo while fathers' heads are crushed
like brittle stone and mothers' bodies are torn open
by monstrous attackers, children they, all written
off as lost Africa, which will remain lost for the next 100
days as it has for the past 300 years. It's a tell of people
my age when you hear us say, I've seen this before,
Camelot and the revolution just around the corner.
Today my around the corner is the Fine Fare,
where I pick up milk, orange juice, and peanut butter
for my girls before getting back to work.
I'm lucky to have work, I've heard a dozen people
tell me in the past week. The Dominican check-out girls
have no union, though surely they thirst for something
greater. I can't know. I don't speak their language.
I am one of those who has sat at the bar with his whiskey,
whispering to himself on an unchosen night, *I was born
too late*, thinking I might have liked to have lived through
the Depression and now it looks as if I will get my wish.
But will I get my FDR? No I will get my Obama,
the first president to have a name that begins with *O*.
O, Obama, be not the chosen, but the unchosen

of the unchosen revolution, not around the corner
but here on St. Nicholas Avenue where the swollen tribes
of unchosen are chanting, *Africa come home*, and raising
their sunbroad arms to demand you be what they believe
you are.

LESLÉA NEWMAN

Prayer for a President

At the first ball
on the first night
the first black president
and the first lady
danced the first dance
while Beyoncé sang "At Last."

At last this day had come
At last this day had ended
At last he held her in his arms

and they were spinning around the dance floor
elegant as the earth spinning around the sun

And just for a moment
she was just a woman
in a fancy white dress
dancing with her husband
and just for a moment
he was just a man
in a crisp black tuxedo
dancing with his wife

and I was just one more American
sitting in front of my TV
wishing this first day and night
could last forever as I danced
myself up to bed, the prayer
I'd been murmuring since morning
spinning around my head:

keep them safe
keep them safe
keep them safe

REBECCA WOLFF

The Most Famous Man in the World

day 12

Are you like me
jug ears
of purpose
defined positively
by your positive
action and the clear vision
toward a common

sense? It's just
common sense. I
feel you. You feel

me. At least one other
in this whole world
famous
to make ready
in the event.

MATTHEW ZAPRUDER

Sad News

day **13**

We have some sad news this morning
from Mars. But I'm thinking about lions. Someone
said something salient and my head became
a light bulb full of power exactly

the shape of my head. Sinister thoughts
at the Xerox machine. A chat with a retired
torturer. Now the sharp blade. Apparently
some solar wind pushed a few specklets of actually

not red but gray Mars dust through the seal
into the vacuum where the very tiny oiled hydraulics
of the light from the distant future collector seized.
What was it my brother said to me once? Like

a vampire bat on a unicorn Change rides
every moment. Houston is full of dead elephants
and empty labs experimenting on silence, open any mouth
and out blows some hope in a binary data stream.

14 *day*

Praise for the Inaugural Poet, January, 2009

Perhaps it's an impossible task
On an impossible day. A young poet
Fixes her gaze along the plaza,

Looks this latest version of America in the eyes,
Looks in the camera at all the places we've touched
Or torched.

Sees who's come to this roll call:
The out of the woodworks, the I never even dreamts,
The I never thought I'd live this longs.

Stands in the sharp report of weak January sun.
The poet probably knows
This family is hers.

The poet probably knows
Before she cuts history to forty-three lines,
Before the capitol has more proof
Of what bullets and ropes couldn't stop,

She has to straighten her back. She needs to take
A deep breath. A black woman is here.
All the black women in her are here to sing.

CAROLINE KLOCKSIEM

Do-Over Like Sky

for Steve and Ezra

—Under which in Iraq sand flies pop like confetti, cotton in ears to lock them out. Woodside sings lullabies to Declan in his head at the same time as Kate back home hoping in her robe.

Ezra in Afghanistan dreams of expensive oil paints, writes to Fay *When I get back I'll paint you the best apple I ever ate and plant an orchard in Washington, crowned with rubies.*

Dear friends—I've put together a package for each of you, and a duplicate I'm sending to the whole wide world.

I bought you this magazine with tits on the cover for the sheer American "because I can" of it. And pure sugar Pixy Stix to fling like streamers into crowds of children. I have to tell you

about the white stock boy at Winn Dixie who saw my pin and whispered to me did I think we'd win. The way he looked around before. And I don't know what all I said to this kid, just stunned by his flaring red cheeks and secret hope.

I'm sending wild rose petals, just in bloom. And this painting more real than the news to show what's waiting back home for you—

RACHEL ZUCKER

Dear Mr. President, I Thought You Should Know

It's February and the wind's so bitter
my toddler, in the front pack, slides his hands
under my armpits and buries his face in my scarf.
I'm sorry to report that some people are still nasty
on the number 1 subway and my son's teacher
has acute leukemia. I don't expect you to change
everything or for everything to change. But every day
it does. My older boys, with their heavy school bags,
struggle to remain standing as we jolt along
these old, old tracks. Someone offers me a seat
but I can't reach it. Someone else won't let me past.
Later, I'll nurse the baby, write some poems, and wait
to hear if the swab I twirled inside my cheek predicts
my bone marrow might save anyone. Until then, I'm held
upright by the press of your citizens, the city's embrace.

Last Migration, a Dead,
Common Yellow-

throated warbler was lying on a stepping stone
in the garden as if presented.
Should I have felt guilty

for washing windows? Should I've
detuned my banjo in mourning
& suspended the stars

until further notice? The fat cat a puddle
in an old, gross chair, I sang. Seasonally
hoarse, my singing

was suddenly accurate. I livened up. The sun
went down unromantically for once.
The birds kept it down.

But what of the world a year from now?
Eight? The last seemed endless,
but we're small. Mayflies

are allowed to say that cut daisies
seem endless. Still,
on election night,

I felt an urge to yodel. I livened up.
If it weren't so unemblematic,
I'd've fired guns at the air.

Last night was an asshole of a night.
Too cold for our hound
to pee. But

we get another. This is where the winter
fat gets converted as we inch into
the disgusting river.

An evening's worth of crows rescinds
at once from the bank
of bald trees

& the sound is of leaves. Against the sun,
the silhouettes, redundant.
I'm surrounded

by nightmares. I misread J. P. O'Connor's poem
". . . the wind that bursts / open puppies
in an endless field." A train

calls by as comforting as a song about trains.
I liven up. The water scales skyward,
through my wool suit,

worn for just such a scene, sharpening
my breath & sending my genitalia
into distant meditation.

I liven up. I look around at us, suddenly
mobile, braving each step,
& I try to give this

all a name. The plastic chandelier
in my head pulses
with the strain.

COLE SWENSEN

Taking Cover under the Sun

what salt of aegis   and salt of rind   when a sky, proportioned
to a flailing cuff. this much done   and augur of

a man walks his dog slowly through the snow   on the radio
one more sense of rain

over time   the brittle acre   white in answer, answers blind
will unwind   like the clock at the center of a cell

a man walks alone through the cold. I wonder what it feels like to know
that approximately half the world has a crush on your husband

whose hand on the lightswitch   of particles filtering down through sunlight
and the sunlight in an empty room coming home.

LAUREL SNYDER

The Greatest Public
Works Program

You're passing
some shitty little
town lost along
the drear interstate.

In a dim afternoon
downpour—
with no gas, no
phone, no family.

Windows open
because the car.
Because the fogged
windshield hates you.

Wet and watching
your map lift suddenly
from the dash, whip
through a slick window,

away, away, away,
sodden, useless, gone
forever in the gray
been left behind—

And that's the moment
you face the road,
the constellation of
ahoy and already,

see the map waiting
beneath your tires.
That's when a swell, a rising,
the promise of there.

That's when you know
ahead will be else, other,
at least not *here*. Maybe
even dry, with coffee.

That's when, driving
on fumes, tired
past gone, you notice
the sky pink up.

The rain lifts, clouds
scatter, and you suddenly
remember—Hope
has no rearview,

can't live in memory.
Hope wakes starving
in the storm,
to off and hunt.

CATE MARVIN

Song of the Bad Bank

Relieve me of my worst asset: my trust
is my beneficence, my benevolence my
trust. Turn those warm arms around me
electric eel, or appeal to my tenderness,

then unfurl me leaf by leaf to hoard me,
make me your bank's bad treat, treat me
to your bad bank, tend to me as you tend
your legal tender, tenderly, till I oscillate

like a pendulum. Bleed me? An entreaty:
We are trying to save you from yourself.
Oh, do not heed me, do not cough a coin
up from your love's coffers. No one ever

loved *me* enough to save me from myself.
Yet every place swarms with beggars. Take
pity, stock my larders with your grief: Do
not bleed me! Feed me, feed me, feed me.

MICHAEL DUMANIS

Occasionally, I Write a Poem

The lust I had for Hot Stuff, she for me,
could not outlast the Bush administration.
I take it personally, who do not take
disasters well. George Bush, my heart
break is your legacy.
The half-wit chaperone of our affair,
you leapt with us into motel room beds.
We were afraid of opening our mail,
owed several banks a hundred thousand dollars.
We thought that we would never see the day.
We didn't. I still feel you on my neck,
Mister Ex-President, like night sweat.
Cleveland is listless. Everything's on sale.
I loiter in the liquidated mall.
I know I treated her the way you treated
the American people, and for that I am sorry.
I have nothing to say about the new president.

MAJOR JACKSON

A General Theory of Interest & Money or Getting the Country in Bed

Stimulus from the Latin *stimulo*:
meaning to goad or to prick is for guys who know

to dance in Elkhart, Indiana,
who suffer no fata morgana,

who make collective nations quiver
so monetary funds deliver,

who finger purses, wallets, online
accounts, have us secrete divine

amounts, launch us into a retail haze,
who desire a kiss of our 401Ks

who whisper and caress their package plain,
less erotic to overfed brains,

like investing in road infrastructure,
or flirting with hi-tech-preneurs.

Not beholden to the notion of trickle down,
these guys evoke boom town

muscular contractions.
Without immediate action

to handle the nation's crisis
with proven Keynesian tactics,

this bedroom of deepening disasters
will lead no doubt to faster, better

layoffs, layouts, lay-ups,
bankrupt, significant cuts.

Stimulus from the Latin *stimulo*:
meaning to goad or to prick is for guys who know

you must pay to play. You must arouse the crowds.
You must stroke the blokes. You must morale the gals.

You must turn-on perform. You must check your technique.
You must ignite the fright. You must bank your rank.

You must strong pitch the rich on Capitol Hill
to support the applause of your Senate Bill.

ERIN BELIEU

H. Res. 23-1: Proposing the Ban of Push-Up Bras, Etc.

So it goes: the garment drops and
               the ladies are busted,

those old carpetbaggers slouching South.

        Oh America,

we don't mean to disappoint,
             but every lover comes with

      a fulsome jiggle, some pudding packed
in the U-Haul, a mole we try to believe

        could be seen as a beauty mark.

But honestly,
       isn't the honeymoon the boring
          part? All that lying about!

And what is beauty but the absence
of symmetry?

        Better to forget
perfection, to remember we were born

     a nation of blemishes,
        a posse of strays with cellulite.

If Benjamin Franklin
       were alive today,

       you know he'd be working a thong
and roller blades on Venice Beach, flying

     the freak flag just beneath Old Glory!

America, it's time to unsuck our bellies
        and show our ugly asses.

We must learn to want each other
       in direct sunlight,

no more or less than what we really are.

CRAIG MORGAN TEICHER

When the Real American

When the real American
language said *together*,
somehow we heard *against*.
We couldn't tell whether

it ever said just what it meant.
We heard *free*, almost inadvertently,
when it said *surveilled*. When we talked
and voted, we defined *irony*.

But the words spoke in earnest,
though each is its own opposite.
Meaning's made in ears, not mouths, but
that's more than words expect us to intuit.

DAVID LEHMAN

February 12

You can see it again but not as close
as midway between earth
and no place faster than you can lose
a foot race to reach a new birth

of freedom where with pensive tread
we ranged across the fields of light,
the hollows and hills we visited instead
of memorizing the Bill of Rights.

Yet how rare the sad tall guilty mute
giant appears and nothing remains
of what raised him above a brute.

Nothing remains except the roar
of the angels and the crimson stains
of blood on the frame of the door.

Hoi Polloi

There were seven of us eating enchiladas at the Casa Romera when Tony Papadakis stood up in the middle of the restaurant, raised his fist and shouted *Obama is a man of the fucking hoi polloi!* We all stopped and stared as he left, the door swinging behind him.

Who are the hoi polloi? Sarah asked. No one was sure. Three women thought the hoi polloi were the rich, sort of like the hotsty totsy, and three men said the hoi polloi were the poor. We all agreed that being a member of the hoi polloi was not a good thing.

Does that mean we love men to be rich and women to be poor? I asked.

No, Steve said. *It means it's best to be neither-nor. We Americans love those who take the middle path. Sort of like Goldilocks, we want to find the bed or bank account that's not too big or too small, like the bowl of porridge that's not too hot or too cold.*

But Goldilocks was a burglar and a thief, Molly argued. *Which is something both the rich and the poor are accused of being from time to time. They're always taking from others what doesn't belong to them. Feeling entitled. Making themselves at home in a world that doesn't love them.*

Tom disagreed. He said the hoi polloi are the average men and women, the kind no one wants to be. They're the faceless masses, the passers-by, like the extras on movie sets. They're designed to look so familiar that no one notices them. Their job is to be everyone in general and no one in particular so that the heroes and heroines can star in their own lives, forever enjoying the distant sound of our applause.

DIANE WALD

Nonromantic Obama Valentine
for America, February 14, 2009

 *day* 27

let us just make a note of one thing before traveling too far on:
obama eats the camera.

in every single photograph where he is smiling
the presidential teeth
require a taming of light, a scrooching in of every aperture
so the picture is not too far bedazzled.

in honor of this i send all america this nonromantic obama valentine
     command:
thou shalt smile!

for our president
is smiling.

just a man.
openly smiling.

not smirking.
not leering sneering grinning or baring clenched military teeth.
not snickering dickering
lying through pearls
not hooting snorting cackling or falling
all over himself like a word with a back-assward meaning or
a sentence all twisted up in itself
like pretzel dough gone wacko in the oven.

and if you have seen him in person you will say
he verily streams with wide openness
with a wild candor worthy of walt whitman
and no one is afraid.

let him beam.
let his raw laughter flow where the fruited plains have faded, have dried.
let them slowly soak it up, that nurturing laughter.
let all the hillsides bloom with colors that no one's seen for eight long years.

let obama laughter ring. long may it.
let it flood the high skies and tie sparkling wonder all up in a silvery bow
like aretha's magnificent inaugural hat!

let the hearts that illumine this day of the pagan saint val
start throbbing anew, start pulsing
in a sweetly smiling america. well of course

we can't pull all that off every day. and surely
we can't ignore oceans of sadness and need
when they're flooding in all around us. but sometimes

we can smile again in america and now at least we have
a person in the white house who knows honestly how to do it.

At the Save the World Breakfast

the White House forward allies begged to ordinary
foundered face objections got and tightly fraught
with legislative Sunday morning
when the breakfast passed with future skies
in policy blue after the rollout tenderness
the eager incapacity of the real to disoblige
one's prescient forbears of concern
of loving's yesterday a lack of sleep, forbearance
to reform green element darling first year
elocution modes rely on closure to prevent
one's aides from tripping after one unsteady kiss
on light perfume of daylight tired throat performance
held the market as it fell across his chair, the country
off entirely eating weakened expectations on the broken
backs of sofas with the Someone's Out There rescue plan,
a householder whose water income severance
waits for no man's one hand finds in close halls court
intensive of the lot, the congress smiling with its apples,
tactic engineers at breakfast loving to resurrect the flowers
ides of confidence in his oath reform adjusting keys
for doors whose open state relies on that neat knife
closing on the loaf writ from the future edge
of buttery admonition, after all a plan took more than hours
or days with eyes across our backs blind total
to ensure the stimulus fluffs its hair like a memorial
to history, wherein tomorrow he'll breathe out
soft again and try his hand at Monday, facing spin
return on protectionist America that wears a fashionable
new cloak stitched from blue umbrellas when the sun
shone cold comparing one man at breakfast with the lonely
trade winds on approach, one's whole body as earthquake
to affairs, a rapt comparison when ties are put on necks
to prove the throat's constricted life beliefs,
short thinking's bread plate put up unilateral to a risk without

provision for a febrile wish, a solution without question
he has to fetch himself from his admirers
with body noises while the game set rules go down in dozens
orthodox, wherein we frame the months with tremor
portents all the way from Valentine's lost cabinet
to the beds and tables whereon tender bodies fetch
as gain and aperture the House whose own first choices
train the face whose mirror has a thousand keeps
and civil animals unrest for urging selfhood to cut down,
realizing all the guys have you tied up with paper threads
whose works will cusp in balance on that still
he is getting up in the morning sigh re-shape the world (again)

BRIAN TEARE

Citizen Strophes (Oakland)

The way he used to polish an apple
against his palms,

the man turns his face in his hands.
The other man knows

a shine can't be convinced
from the skin of this

grief : he won't look, as in
to cut, the caesura of it

a swerve through nerve to bone a deep
end stop.

Neither is lucky
walking away from the other because

to walk again as singular
is to ask for tenderness from the grid.

Avenue to avenue
all day for weeks he's noun to noun and the ground of the specific

shimmers, the median —
thistle, plastic bag and glass, asters — collects

the bright trash of months
lacking rain, dust

the sum of a terrific meanness. "He" walks
through the city in the poem

because I need help, a place
to put questions, each query

a little white card dropped through a slot
I cut in the democratic

pronoun. A response?
It doesn't feel

like a Monday.
I don't know

what it feels
like. All I know is

he's so depressed he's
me : lovelorn, jobless, a lot of uninsured trouble

with teeth and vision, as in :
sidewalks seem longer

under construction in midday sun :
delay, brake, bumper, hit-

and-run's smashed glass crackling
on the crosswalk, hark

the commuter's two syllable song :
fuck you! The prosodic power

of spondees, an afternoon's refrain,
the stylist saying

I don't drive anymore. Drivers
carry too much anger,

and her customer, *I wouldn't either but*
he won't let me take the baby on public transit.

Meanwhile : he's thinking there's no way
the city's going to beget tenderness

anytime today;
I'm thinking lines will lie down

one on top of the other again
and touch just

so : most intimate
where they break :

separate, wary
as the man on a milk crate by the ATM who yells

The whole war needs to be balled up and burned
with all the money

then stops to size him up
and say :

You're one fat fuck.
Is this what a citizen feels

like? Sticky fresh asphalt
hot in the nostrils,

I only know he's on foot
when he sees the deer

panic in the parking lot near the highway.
Startle, dart,

it runs between cars, shopping carts,
it runs out of the lot the wrong way up the off ramp

from the highway, runs so close by
he sees its thin ears flash translucent

pink in sun—
tenderness—before it vanishes

in a crash of traffic.

I Think You Are a Good Manager

So, how did you like
our session the other day?

So, let's go over
the results.

We don't think that
personality changes over time.

There is no right or wrong
personality.

But we can make you more
aware.

So I talked to M.
the other day.

Boy, do you have
a fan.

He
praised you.

He
praised your creativity.

He
said he very much enjoys

talking to you.
He

said you are an
excellent communicator.

He
said you are

a pleasure
to work with.

He
really is

your biggest
fan.

But now, O.,
the one thing he

was worried about,
the one thing that he

told me is
he

worries you are
straitjacketed.

He
said there were no

behavioral problems.
None at all,

but that he
worries you are

straitjacketed.
Because I want

to let you know
that there is

nothing wrong
with you.

Nothing is wrong
with you at all,

but there are people
who are like the cops.

They will enforce
the rules.

Now let me ask you
something,

do you think
you are in a political

environment?
Do you think

that there are
people around you who

manipulate
a situation?

There are people
who are like the cops.

They will enforce
the rules.

Right now, I think
we need to work on

influencing behaviors, on
influencing others.

So, let's go over
the results.

We don't think that
personality changes over time.

There is no right or wrong
personality.

But we can make you more
aware.

Now, you are kind of
a live and let live sort of

person, but these people,
O., these people

don't know where you're
coming from

and they don't care.
You want my gloves-off

and honest opinion is
I think there is nothing wrong

with you.
We need to work on

influencing behaviors.
I think we should talk about

managing colleagues,
peers, people who don't have

your best interests at heart,
and managing M.

I think, as a manager,
I think you are

a good manager.
I think we should talk about how

to keep the alpha males
who don't know what they are

talking about
from railroading you,

from thinking you don't have
a spine, and to keep M.

from talking over you.
There are people

who are like the cops.
They will enforce

the rules. Are you willing to be
more political, to learn how

to influence?
Have you thought about

confronting M.?

Poem for Comrade Duch

day 31

What choices do I have
And how will the student be graded
And how will we know that the student work is good enough
And how will we know that it is the best possible work
If the grade is meaningless
If the choice is meaningless
It's not a choice it's a student
And it's meaningless
Where then do we look for meaning
What slips from the lining of the lung
And collects in the ruts of the field hospital
Mashed up with grass and mud
In the box is the fetid dictator
Going south in his agebox
Going south in his box of hair
The body of judgment has been assembled
And has been disabled by the war on terror
And is a disabled box
In the box the choices are limitless
In the box the choices are meaningless
I've made a target mask for the dictator to wear
I've made a shirt of greaves and a shirt of shrivening
I've made a script for the dictator to cite
But the dictator is wearing so many shirts he can't speak
He's inside the box without so much as a diktat
And now without a dictum I'm rammed with my éclat
I'm rammed with my école
Which is an école normal superior and without meaning
On the outer back of the dictator is the hare shirt
With fists in his hands and a mask of a grass hare
Where is the garden grate to look through
Where is the guarded gate
Where is the garden that marks the horrorshow from the orphanage
The horrorshow from the horrorlogium

On the face of the medieval town
Mechanical girls are made up to strike the time
The girl who is the mayor, and the girl who is the butcher
The girl who is the sower, and the girl who is the soldier
The girl who is the swayer, and the girl who is the reaper
The girl who is narcotic, and the girl who is the nun
Strike up this band of little girls
Strike up the gastric band
It's time for a dumb show, a clown show
Where is the grill of the dictator
Where is the minstrel grill
The ministry of minstrelsy
At that gate at that gate
I rehearse my mute expression
I rehearse my spiritual advance
I tape my damp flyer to the gate
I tamp up my dape fier
I tape my dome flape
I dlape it
and dlope
There
Where
Rain collects on the tape like blank eyes
And collects somehow under
As if the tape had udders
For a chemical raid
The air makes itself a blank tape whips and hisses
Spits I want to look him in the mask
I want to hear his anima cry
As he slumps on the guards' shoulders
And the guards shrug him off like the shit of centuries

Skulls Are So Last Year

(including half a line by Thomas McGrath)

Unattended money may be searched or destroyed

Woman in the doorway of Dunkin' Donuts
reciting *will you help me get*
something to eat will you help me
get something to eat will you
help me get something
painful revision of WCW's
modernist syntax of insistence

Please hold on money is leaving the station

In New York at five past money
many small vacancies open

Debt clock broke down whirling exhilarating
proliferation of zeroes we just don't have
that many light bulbs

Do not accept money from persons unknown to you

In New York at a quarter past money
I'd put my queer shoulder to the wheel if I could find it

Be careful when opening money as contents may have shifted

Put my shoulder to the wheel but I'd go tumbling
through the absence of value to the lack of a floor
flat on my face in this fiction of a symbol

That can itself be sold
or you can sell the absence of the symbol
bundle the absences and divide them among a multiplicity
build a whole towering extravagance

Something like the way in Tallinn this month
the Estonian Philharmonic is holding a Festival of Perfect Silence
so we are planning to celebrate the completed

Vanished tower of abstract money

A little reminiscent of that fading fashion for vertical foods in restaurants
an edible structure that would allow your meal to rise from your plate
toward you mirror of an entire economic architecture shimmying upward

Into the thinning atmosphere the most tenuous needles of money

And maybe why today the barrista who's charging me
do you want cash back with that
wears around her neck a cameo
no antique but sly parodic black oval
upon which a coral-red skull and crossbones are looming

That's why skulls were everywhere last year
on jeans pockets backpacks wallets china your wristwatch

Sign of piracy

Would you like another transaction

What People Say

The Dalai Lama says be kind whenever possible, then,
     remember it is always possible.
My son says Simon Says:
     and waits for you to be Simon
and is happy for a moment if you take the cue to lead
     but when he is doesn't differentiate
between a noun and a verb and so
     might say Simon Says Cat, which may mean meow or lick
but not, say, pose regally. That doesn't say cat.
     The command has been rearticulated here
in ways that surprise me every day
     and it's no joke that it's startling now
to hear someone speak well
     even speaking well of those who do not deserve it.
Even challenging ideas of what it is to deserve.
     Who remembers in each moment what is possible.
The commander-in-chief has, in his first act as such,
     authorized 17,000 more troops to Afghanistan
and Karzai's spokesman says "We have opened a new page."
     We have paged a new open we have known an open page. We turn
and I find that I want to speak better
     and isn't it something that he quoted *Swing Time*
in his inaugural address, in which Fred & Ginger sang
     pick yourself up, dust yourself off.
What is it to lead? And not be, as they say, an occupying force?
     He says "I am the eternal optimist.
I think that over time people respond to civility
     and rational argument." And walks away.
Walk away, walk away, it makes me happy for a moment
     to command: Possible! But that's not a verb either.

KATIE FORD

You Are No Messiah

You are no messiah
but we wished for you then

bodies, benzine, lead, mold

behold: our new list of elements
lo: we were afraid
fear not: "you can get your life back
in order"

we feared, we beheld, we lowed
and bellowed as cattle

the city that did and didn't die
begged how much more

can one beg:

"diabetic—two pills left"
"my house is floating"
"there are gas lines that are still spewing gas"

The boats couldn't operate among
"unfathomable things," unfathomable dogs
tangled in live, wet wire

we wished for you

who would have sent
more than a dirge

A Small Gesture of Gratitude

day

for Erin, Adam, Michael, Barack

I have to tell you something. There is an *actor* in the world
called Joaquin Phoenix, and he's been *acting* pretty strangely
lately (messy beard, monosyllables, not promoting random

blockbuster, etc.). Two robots who embody barely one
percent of everything worth hating about the media were
on a 24-hour news channel "analyzing" his "controversial"

interview with David Letterman, a talk show host.
These polished zombies were speculating about "this whole
controversy" under unkind studio lights, quizzing each

other about whether this *actor* is *acting* or actually crazy
or on "drugs"—desperately dry-humping the finer points
of one of the least crucial issues of our moment—

and whether the talk-show host, who all but patented
mainstream deadpan irony, was in fact pissed off
at this *actor* for appearing on his eponymous talk show

and creating a "controversy" that the human lampreys
who dole out the news with coffee spoons could fasten
themselves to, thus escalating ratings, ad sales, etc.

I have to tell you that I was in a public place, scribbling
about this completely irrelevant but also kind of excellent
Warholian non-interview, and at the very moment my pen

was poking into said cloud of pop-culture effluvium,
I overheard two women behind me, talking about the self-
same non-controversy—let's just call it a nontroversy:

*I think it's an act I think he's crazy He's on drugs I don't think
so You don't?* But I can't turn around because I'm afraid
that if I see their faces—let alone make eye contact,

acknowledging in even the smallest way that I am complicit
in the nontroversy—a huge blood-crusted mortar and pestle
will descend from the ceiling and grind my head into a paste.

TV news is killing us and the people who own it are killing us
and the criminals at whose behest they concoct more nontroversies
are killing us and the tons of hairspray and makeup they smear

on the toxic marionettes who mouth nontroversies are killing us,
as is our ignorance of the reality of everyone killing everyone.
If it's true to say the incubus fills us for the succubi to suck us dry,

why shouldn't I? Pointing into bottomless, topless, sideless
madness is what scads of poets do and have been doing all along:
we take facts and/or feelings, herd them like butterflies

into killing jars, then run pins through them for the aesthetic
and/or ethical scrutiny of a tiny audience made mostly of other
butterfly-killers. I have to tell you something else:

I have "invented" and am promoting a neologism
for the perineum: the boyband—as in,
"I'm walking funny 'cause I just had my boyband waxed"—

injecting something useless into the lexicon, if you will;
messing on a microlevel with the zeitgeist, if you won't.
I've been running this new term—the boyband—

by a number of people recently, thus exposing
and/or confirming myself as the frivolous, vulgar idiot
I frequently am or *act* like; but that's the kind of behavior

everyone has come to expect from Americans anyway,
so I am in this sense as American as anyone else.
This poem is turning into a shuddering black hole

of broken rules, much like the Cheney/Bush regime,
albeit silly rules I tend to bray at my students about not
breaking: referring to the poem itself and (worse) to myself

writing it, invoking Penelope and Eliot and celebrities,
hawking awkward similes, referring to "teaching poetry,"
overusing quotes and/or italics, pay no attention to tenses,

not caring whether I've inadvertently stolen
a phrase or an image, deploying the word "reality," etc.
Maybe certain poets should have breathalyzers

connected to their computers or typewriters or hands
so they can't do what I'm doing right now to this poem.
Next week, if I accidentally meet President Obama

because someone I adore performs an amazing feat or merely
something "controversial," gets invited to the White House,
needs a plus-one, figures I'm good for a laugh, brings

me along, and I get 15 seconds of face time with
our new commander-in-chief, I'll just fuck it up: forget
to mention Prop 8 or Darfur or health care or education,

instead squawk some idiocy about how I've decided
we should all call the taint the boyband or hey,
what about that Joaquin Phoenix, so crazy! Maybe not

as scandalous as Grace Slick, a singer, who came this close
to dosing Richard Nixon, another president, with LSD, a drug;
but either way, whether Obama cracks up laughing,

high-fives me and says, *Yeah, but what about the girlgroup?*
or has the secret service 86 me, or barely blinks and moves on
to the next guest, some perfect mound of reptilian excrement

like Rush Limbaugh will catch wind of this non-event and funnel
it into one of his flatulent Hindenburgs of "controversy,"
so folks can be distracted by "that whole boyband thing,"

or christen it Taintgate—once a thing has a -gate, you can stop
calling the thing "that whole ——— thing"—and I'll take
only this notoriety to my early grave. Nonetheless, I'll be known

for something—like Penelope, who loomed, or Orpheus, who lyred.
By the way, thanks for nothing E. Spitzer, R. Burris, T. Daschle,
R. Blagor;asld,gkjp—at least S. Palin isn't, at the time of this

concocting, melting our collective American face off
with her down-home hubris, end-times agendas and meth-
cooking, wolf-killing kin. Has anyone else come up

with the phrase *lipstick on a Dick* yet? Probably—I call
it The Anxiety of Coincidence (see above for annoying
tics). So much to do, so many rules to redo. But now,

my beloved friend who takes me to the White House,
unwitting kindling for the media blaze, I tell you
this: I'm sorry. Also, you're welcome. And to those

witnesses who prefer to be protected from poems
and butterflies, I tell you that I'm sorry some insidious force
led you here, but that you, perhaps most of all, are welcome.

System Error

We are sorry for the inconvenience.
There has been a problem with the database.
An internal error has occurred
or there may be too many users on the server.

There has been a problem with the database
but you made a prettier constitution
or there may be too many users on the server.
We cried when you spoke clearly

but you made a prettier constitution.
We believed in your honesty
and we cried when you spoke clearly.
We may have lied about our habits

but we believe in your honesty.
Our last days as children
we may have lied about our habits.
Ask the family about their home

or our last days as children.
An internal error has occurred—
ask the family about their home,
we are sorry for the inconvenience.

TODD FREDSON

Air and Simple Things

'Tis a gift to be simple,
'tis a gift to be free . . .

It is not the bird that is beautiful
but the sudden scale it gives to the field—

like that unexpected instinct toward fatherhood,
little receipt
for the silliness a child can make of the world.

This innocence, mixed with the fright
of passing—

daisies have filled the pasture
since the horse's death

and warp in unison
with the breeze. Pushed one way, held down
swaying back around.

They pop up like a ball held under water.

The swallows dive from the wire as I pass,
row of boys playing shot-in-the-heart, toppling,
hands clutched to their chests . . .

just in time, the swallows glide out.

All of this fluttering.

The stalwart shadows
and their branches
tangle on the side of the barn.

Washed-out boards slant
while the elms have grown taller

to mark that space,

the projection and the boards like two wings lathering—no, knees, to
grass seed,
racing
to not lie down first.

Ehhhbb, Ooo, Oommmoo, Eeeooooooooooo

You are a sad bear. A homeless suicidal bear. I want to tell you to not give up on yourself but there is no reason why. I hug you and wish you good luck.

The device is a microphone. You must speak into it. Wash your face first. Abruptly stare into the crowd. Backlit. Stars and shadows. Squint the eyes. The nation is in a state of crisis.

You tap on the window of your cell, pouring poetry only it comes out like "ehb ehb moooo."

[Translation: Madame Speaker, Mr. Vice President, Members of Congress, and the First Lady of the United States: I've come here tonight not only to address the distinguished men and women in this great chamber, but to speak frankly and directly to the men and women who sent us here.]

The nation wants you in several stages: the first, smiling, creased corners of the eyes.

"Eeebbbbbb moo."

[Translation: We will rebuild, we will recover, and the United States of America will emerge stronger than before.]

The second requires a solemn expression, downturned lip, furrowed brow.

"Ohhhh, booo eb, maaaaaaaaaaaaaaaaaaaaaa. Ohbbbbb."

[Translation: My budget does not attempt to solve every problem or address every issue. It reflects the stark reality of what we've inherited — a trillion dollar deficit, a financial crisis, and a costly recession.]

The third would be confidence.

"Oh oh, eb, ahhhhh."

[Translation: We are not quitters.]

Show us that self-assured determination that credit will flow, baby, oh yeah that's it. The nation has a hard-on.

You point to the meal tray and explain how the x- and y-coordinates of the points surrounding the coffee-cup stain would be satisfied under the equation $x^2 + y^2 = 28$.

[Translation: Our nation needs better health care, education, renewable energy sources. A massive recovery effort is on the way and every bank will not be nationalized forever.]

"Obama looks Reaganesque today," the nurse says.

"Reaganesque?" I say.

"In that he looks confident," he says.

"Ehhhbb, ooo, oommmoo, eeeooooooooooo. Ehhhhhbbb, eeeem, oooob, beeeeeoooo, obbbbbb."

What will happen to you, bear, when you are released?

Ebb, oh, ebb.

Behind the Barracks, after the War

God said, *quit your crying.* God said, *I stopped the planes, I closed the base,*
I turned out the lights, what else do you want?
And down from the mountain, not smoke, but a delicate wind the likes of
    which
we only half-remembered,
and God said, *I saved some cities, I doused their flames,*
and God said, *I waved away the smoke so you could breathe.*
And on their delicate necks, new flowers swayed in the postwar breeze
so the field smelled sweet and strange,
and *here is a hand grenade,* God said, *hollow, harmless. Here is a Remington*
    M24
bolt-action, also empty—
and it's true the fields stopped burning after a while,
and it's true he had enormous arms,
and *you live in a free country,* he kept saying, invisible behind the apple
    tree's
burst of petals, *at ease,* he said, *here is your mortar,*
take it home and keep it, here is your nightfighter, here is your interceptor,
take them to your wives, here is your gasmask, here is your repulsion device,
here is your pulsebomb, your smartbomb, your brainbomb,
give them to your children, they're useless now.
And then the wind kicked up and then it was late, a cool and lovely
    evening
after the war, the field behind the barracks exploding with lightning bugs,
my duffel by my side—I was going home at last—and *what's wrong with*
    you?
God said from high above the rooftop. *Cheer up!*

DAVID RODERICK

In Some Places They Held Picnics   *day*

O you chorus of indolent believers,

you abide by no music; you mob, shout, noose

this new voice that could sing. If you succeed, rope

the old tree, we will writhe there kicking, dangling

from our years. In some places they held picnics

where a hanged one remained, unnamed and held high.

Fear this history-making. Feel our drooped arms:

we were lowborn and tangled, grown from white roots

that for years lived off black soil. Understand? Don't

think that most didn't see and take advantage.

Even children saw, played beneath the sculpture

petrified while it swung: the day's kept body.

It's so cruel, what history's done, yet we know

now how true a new voice can be when made bold

by a crowd, though some feel the tree still swinging.

JOSHUA MARIE WILKINSON

Poem for Barack Obama

Ten envelopes & forty-thousand a
day to go — so here's mine. Funny
to think we thought you'd read

our blog. Forfeiting, tanked
villains on the twitter, & your
coin face on some 1-800
supplies while they last. It's not that

everything got weirder,
it's weird that we're already
used by it.

So, let's see: Have you put
the wars to bed? Did you do
all of our homework?

I know it sounds stupid here, but
I'm sorry your friends aren't to
call you up anymore. There's no way

to talk to you directly, I guess,
so I'll evince that.

It's a poem. (Actually, see *Hughson's
Tavern* if you want to break all the way down
for an evening.)

Since you left town, some
good things have happened:

Rae Armantrout got famous. Noah
got a job. Johannes's comments on
Harriet are still better than tv. *Tuned
Droves* dropped, and it's haunted.

Even Spicer's *Collected* went platinum,
so the ocean's not so tough after all.

Maybe your assistants can help you with
the references. It's just a poem. That's
part of its work to point to other shit. Of

course we want to hear about your kids' dog.

JOHN BEER

My Calamine Lotion

Winter was hard: the whole Judith thing,
I seem to have less underwear than I used to,
or at least it's a chore to keep track of, turns up

in unexpected places, taxicabs, and Chicago
gets fucking cold in January, for reals.
And then I started dating Barack Obama.

IAN HARRIS

Welcome to Hard Times

Carole King on cassette and the shaded lake and the white
boat with a skier skipping along behind it. "You've taken
and taken from your family," saith

your inner voice. You've taken *The Peaceable Kingdom*
to the wilderness and between the skier and the white boat
and the shaded lake, and all the rest of it, there is little to ruin

the feeling. You set out your things to begin
your novel. The failing economy clamors behind the trees.
Your children are bruising around out there in the sunbeams;
you are falling in love with your wife for the second time.

Aspen groves tremble behind her and groves of Doug fir
tremble also. There is quite a lot literature has to say
about your wife. She is standing at the edge of a grove,
or at the mouth of a western river. The failing economy

clamors behind the trees. She is at a party in Sun Valley
and she and you and everyone else is healthy-looking and just in
from skiing, and while she is carrying on about Norman Mailer
and Leo Kottke the meteor shower of nineteen ninety-four

is happening in the cold sky behind her. Geese are working
themselves through the same cold sky. A decade tear-asses
across your body and hers and she is reading *Welcome to Hard Times*

by E. L. Doctorow. The theme of the room is Santa Fe–Sun Valley
and there are zigzag wool blankets and riverstone floors and photographs
of miners standing in creekbeds, long stretches of Mormon country, etc.

Don Henley is on the stereo, or the other Topanga Canyon groups.
"You've got your hair slicked back and those Wayfarers on, baby," etc.
She deserves a richer life, your wife. She grew up enfoliated in blue-green
    water.

It's late afternoon. The lake is thinning of boats. Your children are
not as you supposed they'd be. The wilderness trembles. Don Henley
is on the stereo. "I can see you, your brown skin shining in the sun," etc.

You set out your things to begin your novel. "The landscape
is very empty except for a few barges of granite," it begins.
It goes on for some time, this emptiness.

NICOLE COOLEY

Girl at the River

Let New Orleans be the place where we strengthen those
bonds of trust, where a city rises up on a new foundation
that can be broken by no storm. Let New Orleans become
the example of what America can do when we come
together, not a symbol for what we couldn't do.
—Barack Obama, speaking in New Orleans,
August 26, 2007

Each waterline a seam we want you to sew up.

Each aerial view we want you to refuse.

Each flight over the city we want you to take back.

Each gaze out the plane window cancelled.

★

It's wrong that I want you
to let me stand forever in my childhood,
in the Before,
at the river by my parents' house,
my plastic umbrella edged in pink.

★

Because water's uneven scrawl erases—

★

Yes, the other president preferred another landscape, flagrant and
    gold-lit.
An aerial view made it easier not to imagine Lakeview St. Bernard Tremé

Easier not to touch the landscape. Easier not to slip under the dark pool
formed by the place's new language. Easier not to stop and ask the people

of the city how they live now.

★

Marshy spillover,
of the first fishing camps,

dockside shacks and families,
where water first met sand
and pilings
did not stay anchored,
where only
second stories rose
above the surge.

★

Did you know that after water there is no water,
that the landscape is scrubbed and dry and yellowed?
So many signs, hand-lettered—
we're coming home. We're coming back. No Trespassing.
And no houses anywhere.

★

Each gaze cancelled. Who will see the city?

★

Another sheeted body under a burning egg yolk sun children crying
beside wind-spun green highway signs along I-10 Families with
Styrofoam ice chests Winn Dixie bags mothers cradling babies
running on hot cement over the causeway

that will lead to buses they've been promised

on the other side of the river that will lead to safety maybe Lafayette
    maybe

★

Put this city back together. Signs hand-lettered, hopeful.

★

Take me back to my childhood room, my house by the levee, where
a hand mirror's small glass lake will never rise

or flood or spill.

ERIKA MEITNER

Slinky Dirt with Development Hat

O Mama. Juice. Pile of dirt.
Sand pit where the workers stopped
working. Home is a backhoe

with no keys, silent, yellow. Passing
cars buzz the lots for sale that still
have trees, have liens. Our development

is mid-cul-de-sac. There are half-moons
carved into hills, and when we walk
down the unpaved, unnamed road,

past the upright pipes marking gas
or sewer, there's often a father and son
joyriding on one four-wheeler, sans helmets.

They wave hello and we wave back.
There's bankruptcy court. A promised
swimming pool. There's hope that bounces

down the stairs, slinks away, and hides
under a chair. My son pitches a fit
when we pass a digger and I won't stop

for the excavation; when the other children
sing the alphabet he doesn't join in.
After two servings of milk, there's

water. Farther, further, father.
Mama. Juice. Pile of dirt, he calls
from the car window to the bleached

frames, empty and bowed as a set
of whale ribs, their cupped hands
spilling sand and clay. He presses

his red mitten to the glass and waves
hello to our master-planned community,
the houses that are just like ours, but for

the countertop finish, or optional bonus room
above the garage, or guns in the cupboards
beneath commemorative plates, tucked

next to receipts for winter and re-wear
that coat one more year. In the dusk,
the mountaintops flatten themselves

to escape the calcified bulldozers
that won't come after them anymore.
It is March and there's snow crusted

over with ice. Our jackets are too small,
but the snaps still snap. The zippers still
zip. We shiver and turn the heat up.

ALLISON JOSEPH

Conservative Love in the
Age of Obama

Meghan McCain complains online: she can't
find a good boyfriend, guy who doesn't
want her to don her mother's pearls and smile,

wave like a future first lady. Girlfriend,
get in line, women of all political persuasions
can't find a man—despite those perpetual

E-Harmony ads on every hour selling
soulmate fantasies of lifetime companionship.
In this economy, divorcing couples who can't

sell their houses continue to cohabitate,
homes full of misery cheaper than foreclosure.
So if you must go it alone, count yourself lucky—

nobody's dumping you on TV on *The Bachelor*,
offering you a rose only to snatch it back
in a ratings stunt no one will remember

in six months. I feel for you, girl, when
Rush and Newt are your party's sexiest dudes,
featured hotties at this year's CPAC convention,

things are dire. Maybe Michael Steele
has a son or two you could date—nice
conservative black boys who don't see color—

yours or theirs? You're blond, beautiful,
twenty-something—surely it won't be long
before you land the man of your dreams:

hunky throwback crazy for cuts
in capital gains but who knows
how to blog and twitter, a stud

quick as a Facebook status update.

LINDA BUCKMASTER

Harvest

Spring-strong sweetness, sap
running up maple—tap it.
What can this man do?

ANN FISHER-WIRTH

In Oxford, Mississippi

Despite last week's snow, the daffodils bloom
in the dead winter grass of gardens and curbsides
all over town; even two-days' jackets of ice

couldn't kill them. The Bradford pears and plum trees,
the quince like drops of blood on thorny branches—
I love them, I hang on to the thought of them

when I despair of humans, when one of my students,
for instance, says welfare is for crackheads, and another
that the fix for capital punishment is public stonings

and hangings—*Thou shalt not kill*, a third replies.

I answer: the chainlink fence on that icy hill six years ago,
the guards that ringed the American embassy
when thousands marched in Stockholm, and I wanted to shout

to those uniformed boys, *Put down your guns and join us.*
My shame that year in Sweden at being American.
Watching Powell on TV, as he tried to make the UN believe

those little dark blips of trucks carried weapons
of mass destruction. That day in glistening springtime
when we learned the tanks had invaded Iraq.

Grief has been our mother. Exhaustion and lies, our daily bread.

Yet the daffodils, reiterating sunlight.
When I woke at five this morning, the birds
and wind chimes were singing. The raccoon that lives

in our crawl space scuttered around on the porch,
thumping and shaking the cat-food bowl. I dreamed
I'd forgotten to come back from Sweden, no longer knew

where home was, if I still had a job. But now I know
home is Mississippi—where William Caughy, age 75,
said *Thank the Lord* when I signed him up to vote

in the parking lot at Big Star last October.

And Thadeus Jefferson, age 82: *Ain't never voted.*
Ain't never registered neither. Can't register,
ain't permitted to. Long time gone did time for drug . . .

Then, when I read him the voter rules: *What's that*
you say? Time for drug not on the list? That's good,
but still can't vote. Never did manage to learn how to read.

—*What's that you say? You asking if I recognize 'OBAMA?'*
Yes ma'am, I surely recognize 'OBAMA.'
Let's sign me up, he chuckled, *so I can vote.*

The Water in Which One
Drowns Is Always an Ocean

*If we are to win this struggle and spread those
freedoms, we must keep our own moral compass
pointed in a true direction.*
–Barack Obama

It is the calm and silence that drown us.

Some people can disturb words
with a mere movement of the teeth.

The pouch of the mouth strewn with roses
                        roofed with lost causes.

Pumpkins and habits have a smell
and breath is its beginning.

The womb carries on its shoulders
a beggar wrapped in earth.

                        Absence washes
away love, taking the tint of all colors.

                From the well of envy
the child teaches us to weep.

                Every sickness has its herb.

Heaven is dark, yet quiet and limpid.
Shovels of earth cannot quench a mountain.

Scum rises to the top of the heart.

                        A bubble on the ocean
a taste the teetotaler will never know.

Do not pour on the strength of a mirage.
Do not torture thirst with shallow water.

A merchant in the rain saves only himself.
A shadow that always follows the body.

When your cheeks beg for fever
		you are halfway there.

Habit is the shirt we wear for a midday nap.
Gray hairs its blossoms.

Hope a pearl worthless in its shell.

Death answers: *I have a lot to say
		but my mouth is full.*

Those destined to drown
		will drown in a spoonful.

The tears of strangers are only water.

ANNE WALDMAN

Shadow for Obama

day **50**

                    not without struggle
Coles Country, Illinois
        nearby
tall
grass
prairies
    beech maple forests
            nearby the Embarras & Wabash Rivers

    all natives expelled by law after the Black Hawk War

Abe Lincoln's father used to farm on Goosenest Prairie

& Abe himself (a log cabin preserved nearby) argued
            in Coles Country Courthouse in Lincoln-Douglas debates
    for return of runaway slaves
Abe Lincoln, young railroad lawyer, coming-into-power of his mind, an
    ethos

                        then shift

    Barack Obama, bodhisattva of ethos

 in the lineage   like we say

  while nearby in contemporaneous time launches Kepler
(in honor of he who studied planetary motion)

whose 95-megapixel camera holds
        42 light-sensitive
modules

        largest camera NASA
has flown in space . . .

            & will orbit around the sun 3 and a half years

hunt for planets measuring
tiny drops in a star's brightness as a planet
passes in front of it
   what civilization so largé & strange (Cahokia Mounds)
      transits

lens on a patch of sky   20 moons wide
in the constellations Cygnus & Lyra
search the shadow of planets
      another Woodhenge?

   discover
(breathe in/breathe out)

   humus

not E.T. we're lookin' for, but it's E.T.'s home

distant Earths
   separating science & politics

         in the stem-cell

shadows drop into daylight savings

in a ceremony 11:45 a.m. eastern time Monday
   in the stem of his agenda
            pale blue dots orbit other suns

as embryonic cells morph into any cell in the body

   tissues beyond a slippery moral slope

"tiny human beings with souls" you think?

                    there
                    are
                    no
                    righteous
                    wars

reportedly invited to the White House:
Hatch, Specter, Castle, Feinstein, Harkin, DeGette and
Edward M. Kennedy

bi-partisano

industrious president in the laboratory

my midnight oil . . .

(Charleston, Illinois—Cahokia Mounds near St Louis—Boulder)

The Book of the Dead Man (Day 51)

day **51**

Live as if you were already dead.
—*Zen admonition*

1. *About the Dead Man and Day 51*

It is Day One of the second half of the first one hundred days of a new
    president, and the Dead Man is counting.
The dead man tabulates the war dead this good president cannot
    restore to life.
He counts up the pins in the map where alliances must be reborn.
This dead man is not the writer of *Ulysses* paring his fingernails in the
    background.
The dead man would go if called, he would enter the Halls of Congress
    without disturbing the decay on either side.
He would slide inside with the care of a porcelain potter, hoping to
    raise up an aggregate of minorities.
He would sidestep the partisan princes of darkness and the merchants
    of war.
For the dead man carries his bifocals like Diogenes his lantern.
It could be Woden's day or Mercury's, the Quaker Fourth Day, Ash
    Wednesday or Spy Wednesday when the dead man shows up.
The dead man fancies midweek, Hump Day at its crest.
It is Wednesday, when the way upward and the way downward are the
    same way.
It is March 11, 2009, the fifty-first day of something good to chew on.

2. *More about the Dead Man and Day 51*

The dead man has been newly roused by a president of many colors.
There has been a worldwide lifting of downcast eyes for good reason.
The fog has lifted that hid the systemic violations of law, and the dead
    man feels the ground shifting.
Now the indigent can hope for more than weeping.
For America was ambushed by the vile and the wicked.
Quickly, it was midnight in America, and the chuckle-heads were in
    charge.

The dead man is all for locking bracelets on the guilty.
Let the naysayers wriggle, let the hefty lobbyists go on a diet.
An age of chess and steak has become a time of checkers and soup.
The dead man waits for his nation to heal the sick and teach the young.
He welcomes home the armies that were the playthings of a presidency
   he is well rid of.
He carries the poor to the clinic, and reopens the laboratories.
His is the hope a young president released.
This president's accomplishments will not be cheapened by the
   barking of the far right.
Check back with the dead man in four years.
For after eight years without a past or future, after the infamy of the
   de facto, the dead man may not soon lower his fist.
The dead man is constructing a runway for the perps.

CATHERINE WAGNER

Oh

day 52

In the little painting of love
Is a man repairing a fence.

A little crap love-object
And a too-big church in the background
Near the sea
By a strip of valley
Lit up like surgical tape.

Metaphors can incline one
Toward healing thoughts.
I will have your experience.

The ocean uptaken in the wind
Rolls inland.
Heal, heal, fungus on toe,
Heal, toe.

If I lose this job
[I have other skills?/There are other workers].

If we all lose our jobs
We go to Ocean City
And photograph ourselves
As human pyramids.
My grandfather spent the thirties
Thus on the beach.

Abundant poverty to live in. Many years.

Between you and me is chestbone.
No meshing.
So eat my face for hours.

If a poem is active
Its action aborts in you
As colored light flies into black.

Keeps flying
The light from long ago
Until the night-blockade.

So shut the book.

The man who mends the fence
Imaginary

Leaves a space for the caissons to roll
Down valley from sea.

Let me eat your face, neighbor
Who owns the Bagel and Deli on High
And has two children
Lily and Garrison.

Imperfect Plenty

After the messenger reports that the flesh kept peeling off the woman's
bones like the bark of a pine tree, Medea turns. O delay.

1.

> The good news:

> > bodies

> > not numbered, but named
> > not statistics, small lives

She walked terrified onto the neighbor's porch and grabbed the living baby
out from under the mother's bloody corpse on the porch swing. *They
just were talking, just talking.* Swing. Blood. Body.

Before we begin to walk, the soles of our feet are as soft as that skin on your
inner wrist. Softer.

2.

There are people in the president's voice. There are people. And listening.
Seen. Eyes in the voice.

> > This is good news.

> eruptions

> > not smoldering, but sound
> > not explosions, applause   .

When the person begins, there is no way to ascertain the source of
pleasure.
Mothers call it *smile*   because we know.

I still swallow hard at the sound of your voice.

3.

More good news:

      nothing happened

not ceasing, not ceasefire, not peace, but fewer bodies. a few. O my few.

What the Fates Allow

Niagara Parks Police Chief Doug Kane said the man
"voluntarily entered into the water and refused medical
assistance at the bottom."

1.

Sometimes a plunge is a plunge:
depending on time of day, sleeplessness repeated
seeking bottom.

The world is fabric unraveling, thread by thread
and *Clotho* and her sisters appear to be on strike:

Enough you despoilers of our hearths,
consumers of our children,
disbelievers and betrayers of health.
We won't help you anymore.

So they sit chatting about how the rainbows used to be prettier
And why the old Gods are so useless nowadays.

And while one man refuses rescue in the North
Another murders kith and kin in the South—*Aisa's* list.

Waterfalls are fiercer than we imagine
Family bonds weaker than conventions desire

These voluntary moments of desperation
That mayhem on a sunny day in the sunny South
mirrors our media's advertisements for "domestic" abuse.
The boyfriend vaguely contrite; the girlfriend, nowhere in sight.
Should she return; should he go to jail?
Duet recorded and soon to be released.

Meanwhile teenage girls are beaten daily
Leading to a brisk business at cosmetic counters

2.

Our continent's resources were so abundant;
many nations thrived even as newly arrived Europeans
sacked temples and released horses, pigs, changing
travel, topography, the hunting rights
so carefully negotiated.

Fevers, deaths, the quest for more land, more gold,
an old story made young again in the glass-walled
structures of ravenous plutocrats.

How this experiment in democracy became formidable
And was almost lost in the dust and quiver
Of towers dashed, a crisis fraught for the corrupted
pleasure of a Shakespeare Reality Show
Hal to Henry—but no Falstaff—leaving us with

This moment of scarcity, anxiety and change
Making some of us giddy and hopeful

No president, no matter his heart's strength and his mind's
Obsidian edge can do what we all must do.

Seek *Lachesis'* wisdom. Beg the spinner's forgiveness.
Offer up our desire for a world made whole
With threads from a stronger more flexible fabric,

Illuminated, our future shared differently.

Random Search

to the TSA

Who will in the night unpetaling lose himself in fealty
His crime heartbreaking, confessed and festering

What undresses in the ground, lost in perjury
If you don't understand who will

He's to be tried for the nearly unforgivable sins of naming
ordinary stars after himself, drinking coffee without labor laws

The whole idea is that your life is an understatement
Wishing you could translate your lust, faking like you care

Marking time by the icicle melting from the eave
Dare not swear it, even to save you

Chaste and chastened, he is touched by you
his body changes as he sinks under your hands

The world's opulent answer, his silent umbrage
A submerged body arrows to the surface

Not by intent but because it is buoyant
He wants to save you, wants to save everyone

When you're finished with him, hand him back his glasses
he tells you to renounce meat and demand an end to inheritance

Tells you to recite Arabic in the gate area
What else is left but to be human here

WAYNE KOESTENBAUM

Sick Poem

March 14. Saturday.
I want to write
a political poem
but I've lain all
day sick on the
pink couch. Stomach
ache, fever. Can't
write a political
poem, can't swallow
a Saltine. Finally
ate half a banana.
If I had energy,
I'd put on an LP
of Peter Pears
singing Schumann
lieder. I liked Mark
Bibbins's political
poem about the
perineum. I wrote
a 3-line political
poem about rimming
but won't submit it
to this mighty
blog. When Obama
was elected I
remembered watching
JFK's funeral on
TV. Alive for both
administrations, I
perceive them
as a simultaneous
bouquet. I hope
Obama puts bike
lanes in every

city and banishes
cars. I hope
Obama stays
skinny. I hope
he writes many
more books when
his blessèd reign
ends. My stomach
ache already
feels better:
maybe I'll
manage canned
broth for dinner.
Today is 50°;
stomach ache
and fever preclude
taking a walk
past pine and
maple trees.
Pines are ever-
green. Maples
shed leaves in fall.
The differences
go deeper. I hope
Obama makes
abortion easy
to obtain and free.
Now it's evening.

SALLY BALL

Racial Parable with No Black People

Between the path and someone's wall, most likely upside-down, the
  chollas scatter.
I'm white, and walking Cosmo. The sharp bulbs cluster almost
  self-contained.
The road startles my attention back with a swooping-in of laughter:

a silent electric minibike, weird stealth and sudden chatter,
two riders, girls in ponytails—they're also white, their minibike
  careens.
The girls, preteen, whoosh near, and I flinch and smile, scattered,

disrupted mid-cactus-reverie, tall lady in green sneakers staring after—
"Hey nigger!" She shouted this, at me. What did she mean?
A lark, a joke, suburban insularity? Her cold lean peal of pointed
  laughter

lingers in the empty road, a presence in the air like shifting weather.
How strange. So many questions rise and multiply and intersect
  between
those girls and me. They really yelled that? Merely naughty now? Each
  scatters.

Did what she said have *anything* to do with race? Or was it just
  intent-to-shatter
what I'd presume, expect, of them? I'm curious, and feel the serpentine
undoing of a need—to be myself, to not be anyone. My own perplexed,
  derisive laughter

fails, and leaves a residue of grief, another worry, another thing the
  matter.
All the imaginary money's disappeared, and now imaginary harmony,
  the sheen
of peace. This stupid girl tests meanness knowing it will scatter?
—dissipate into the desert air, confident and flown, like laughter.

Hey, Obama

You're doing the hard stuff today, blocking bonuses, calling out the executives who will have to give up their mansions on Martha's Vineyard (never been) and this morning I understood the magnitude of "The Dow is up six points," so I'm feeling engaged with the political moment; I'm thinking "do the Summers thing" and "do the Krugman thing." I'm feeling all socialist and radical and if I weren't so lazy I'd grow my own vegetables and ride my bike to work. Instead I rail against the talking heads on CNN. I smack down Bill O'Reilly in my head. I smack down Rush Limbaugh in my head. I kick James Dobson in the head even though he's irrelevant because that's how empowered I feel by this moment, Obama.

I also want to find a way to rough up Bernie Madoff because it's like the 80s again when you were a kid and I was a younger kid and we were surrounded by media depictions of Kings of Commerce. You know: pinstripes and *greed is good*. Fur coats and big hair and diamonds. I want to rough Bernie up with kicking and biting, but my chance is gone; he's locked away.

My sister calls because we can get my mother health insurance for one thousand dollars a month. This is because my mother has dementia. This is because she has an upside-down mortgage and no pension. Do you see where I'm going with this? I can hardly believe it myself; like David Plouffe is writing this for you through me. It's hard-core stump material. She's brown, by the way, which could help too if you put her up on a stage with you to sign a paper that said that she didn't have to pay half her wages to be insured. I'd write to Oprah, but I think they would just give her a make-over.

One hundred days. One hundred days. One hundred days. One hundred days. One hundred days.

I wish I were wise or an economist or a butchier Rahm Emmanuel, but I'm not. From where I'm standing it seems like you're an answer, not the answer, but as good an answer this moment might have given us. Obama, I don't even think you'd like me because I'm sort of trashy, but I don't need you to like me. I need that thing you promised, the thing I can't say out loud because I hate sentimentality, am superstitious. Keep that going. Somehow you're keeping it going.

PATRICK CULLITON

Song

Emma is your brain ok did it
slip. The sky has a bunch
of stupid potions. Now your chin

will fit a starling keep it in there
post-stitch. We can sew stars on the fog
house for work. Is your brain

ok Emma did you break a heel
did it slip. It's ok to never
forgive ice the stupid potions.

Quiet Emma
Chicago is quiet with alert
little lights and half rain.

CATHERINE BARNETT

Small Parable for the Sixtieth Day

A man carries an armful of dogwood into the bus,
the branches wrapped in the day's paper,
the news no longer legible or haunting
or obsolete but put to use,
damp, darkened, waterlogged, bleeding
against the early spring cuttings.

AMY LEMMON

Audacious: An Acrostic

day

Here she is: smiling and posed, hand on knee.
Oh where did she get that shirt? Tie-dyed
Pinks and purples swirl into a sparkle-studded heart
In the center of her chest, just above the scar
No one really notices anymore. Someone else
Gave her the sparkly shirt, dressed her in it just

For Picture Day (which I somehow missed). And thank God
Or she would have been in the drab uniform her principal
Requires even of the kids in District 75, the *special* ones.

Could it be that mothering her will always be a series of
Handings-over, letting others more qualified tend, evaluate,
And teach? Who will walk with her when she turns 21 if there's
Not a drop left in the well? What kind of woman will she be—this
Girl who's never heeded No? May her cherry chapstick kisses
Ever find a gentle cheek, all her bedtime stories end with *Best Beloved*.

ARIELLE GREENBERG

Whose Mission It Is Only to Pray   *day*

They might have to shut down the main highway in town this summer, during the height of tourist season, to bring in enormous wind turbines that will arrive by ship from Denmark and truck them to the western part of the state where they will become part of a farm, an industry, a stab of hope twirling whitely in the future to generate clean energy. One city council member asks, "Why don't we just make the wind turbines here, and that way we won't have to ship anything, won't have to shut down the highway, won't have to stop the tourists and their money from coming to town, bring in jobs for all the factory workers recently out of work?" The others laugh, but I am taken with the idea. Why don't we? I keep thinking about it as I make garlic toast, put the eggshells in the compost bin, dress my oldest child.

This is not the beginning of any poem I can think of: wind turbine, city council, highway, garlic toast.

This is not even my life: rural route, farm industry, city council, compost bin.

I live here, I tell people, *but really I live there*. Or, *I live there when I'm not living here.*

The tourist and her money.

For a local project, I'm trying to find poems about food co-ops, about acupuncture, about garbage that I can print up and post in the windows of the shops downtown. All of which are independent and all of which fit on four blocks, which should tell you something about where I'm living. About how I am spending my money, or not.

These days, why don't we write some poems with money in them, and local food, and wind turbines, and city councils? Why don't we?

★

I can't think of how to break a line because I am trying to keep alive the baby who is growing inside me. If I break a line—well, it just doesn't seem to come to me to break that line.

Cathy Wagner sends me Blake's *silken twine* on an army dog tag that she made in Salt Lake City for protection. I wear it, and I wear a Middle Eastern eye emblazoned on a hand on a string of garnets that I made my father buy for me when my first baby was new, and I wear a Mexican safety pin of turquoise and silver and blue thread that my midwife gave me on my underwear. For protection. Every morning I put them on, one at a time, and every night I take them off, one at a time. The nun I meet on the airplane says she will have someone back at her convent write my name in a special book and the elder nuns, whose mission it is only to pray, will pray for me and my baby. I am a reproductive rights advocate but I will take what I can get, and be grateful.

This is not the end of any poem I can think of: *keep the baby alive, keep the baby alive, keep the baby alive*. But it's the poem I have been writing in the wind these past eight months, to generate clean energy. I am sorry there are no breaks in it. I am not sorry.

MENDI LEWIS OBADIKE

Parable of the Lucky Man

I once heard tell of a man who sailed to the heart
of the ocean. He went out all alone in a paper ship.
The gift was that those layers of wafer-thin sheets
carried him safely for years, far from shore,
through rough waters, until one day he hit a rock
that scraped the veneer and punctured the fragile
floor. As saltwater rushed into the ship, and the walls
began to soften, he looked out in each direction.
He saw no land. Only water, water, water, water.

Some might have panicked or made wild plans
of escape, but he thought: *I'm a lucky man*,
and sat down to wait for his miracle. He sank
that way, deeper and deeper, until the ocean
had devoured his body. He began to tread,
with only his head above water. The wonder
was that a raft somehow appeared. It was sturdier
than any transport this man had seen in years,
but still, it was just a raft.

Did he hoist himself upon that raft? Did he lie down
on his back to catch his breath? Did he turn onto
his stomach and begin to paddle? With no land
in sight, did he imagine his best chance was to move
himself ahead, towards the unknown? Did he
figure he'd better not turn back? Everyone wants
to know how the story ends. The kicker is that you
and I are the lucky man. We must row on out,
into uncharted waters, to finish the tale together.

JENNY FACTOR

A Ghazal for Hope

The children of Adam are limbs to each other,
. . . created of one essence. Is that essence called Hope?

I've bent on one knee. My throat wouldn't open.
My eyes couldn't lift. Not even in hope.

Two boys stand alone. The blacktop turns hostile.
One child makes a fist. The other makes . . . hope.

When you were sworn into office, Los Angeles shivered. We
huddled up at night. The cat, and hope.

We were sparing heat, dreaming of a smaller gas bill.
Now the season is turning on a spitfire of hope.

So it's spring on the tarmac. A California touchdown.
First the wheels, then the stop. This end-point is hope.

I've heard, in the dark, the fear in the desert:
You give it all up, you even lose hope.

My mother, the Certified Financial Planner, told me
that markets change direction at the Ides of March. *(Let's hope!)*

And we're marching. We're stomping. We're heading into
a new season . . . of meaning, and worry. A season of hope.

We're making more from less, cooking our mothers' old recipes.
They taste like memory. They taste like Hope.

Deputize the poets to paste truths in empty storefront windows:
a world seen precisely is as precious as hope.

Dorothea Lange, Rod Stryker in 1935
took photos to lift like a fist of hope.

And a man in a chair knew that art bore a meaning,
that to go to the people was an act of hope.

Where there's wheat in a field, there's song in a sparrow.
Who has waded waist-deep through the mudflats of hope?

Measure your health by your sympathy with morning and spring.
That's Walden-era Thoreau. A man versed in hope.

I'll practice my jump shot. I'll round up a street game.
But I'm 5 foot 3. I may need some hope.

This change takes time. I lose perspective.
Hold a psalm in the palm. Let's factor in: Hope!

MICHAEL MORSE

Void and Compensation
(Wizards and Bulls)

In the building called *Verizon Center*,
portmanteau suggesting truth and horizon

and a position not quite left or right,
Barack Obama watches basketball.

An unlikely result, a bad market:
the Wizards are thumping the Bulls.

D.C.'s cellar-dwellers, among the league's worst,
stick it to Chicago's playoff hopefuls.

Hard times, these Bulls—from championship bling
to afterthoughts—post-Jordan, downright bearish.

It was once their market after all.

Double-double: A man watches his new home
blow out his old one, clapping politely for both.

The Wizards crunch numbers. The Bulls can't rally.
Caron Butler goes baseline, goes glass. A bank.

Antawn Jamison keeps cashing dividends,
nothing but net, his classic fall-away.

One must have a mind of autumn
To regard the twos and treys
Of the pure-shooters entrusted with show.

★

If a wee ball dancing on a jet of water
in a London shop window inspires

Yeats's meditation on Innisfree,
his gem of imaginary dreaming,

let an orange ball above a rim
inspire us and be our bonus:

the backup center for the Wizards throws down
and salutes his new commander-in-chief.

And one, cries the color commentator
who knows that games proceed in stops and starts,

doldrums and flurries, deficits and runs
with reserves who might cut gaps when starters

lose their leverage, fall into foul trouble.
You need a sixth man to stay competitive,

a little security with time lines
and shot-clocks and quarters that wind down.

But all the small transgressions add up:
hand-checks, reaching in, the push down on the block.

In the finance of fouls, excess
yields, not earns a bonus situation:

I lament the air-balls and bricks of insurers
and miss their Stockard Channing voice-overs

and wonder why they're in a bonus situation.

★

I don't get the derivatives they speak
of in the dying print of newspapers—

I don't get the long and the short of it,
the trading and the lack of transparency.

We clearly feel better about lending
when the lexicon is one of games played,

of steals and assists, of Peter and Paul.

In a collective of social fundamentals,
of moving the rock and clamping down on D,

do we elide the terms of our occasion
or call out our card-carrying trouble?

The regulators in gray, black, and white
are whistle blowers some love to hate,

keepers of the key, mercilessly booed
yet necessary ideas of order.

Barack, I'm clapping for you:
Glass of optimism, bank of good will

and soft rim, let the stars soar and not
the kites, no bad checks as floats or figures.

New man, genuine fund, carry my vote.
I wish you godspeed among the game-players.

SARAH VAP

Against One Another Like Glass

day **66**

When I need him,

will a paranormal Jesus
come to me and will I love him

like the poet, David—a residue

of stars to express
what is lost in this and how

can this be imagined: experiments
on the scale of this world.

The saddle-shape of all
of outer space over his shoulder bent

warmer, wetter, perhaps

than we'd expected. Pull the girth solid around

this naked specificity

of world,
and around his human body—until our history

becomes apparent. I have, even now,
less hope.　　　　The stakes are still uncreated

in his childhood-time. Supernatural

is beyond nature.

But magic
is of the Magi.

BRENDA SHAUGHNESSY

Citizen

I could never quite entirely
believe anything, sadly.

Even the many million leaves
belong less to their trees

than to their kind of tree,
and to October.

This past October was maybe
the last truly scary

Halloween. The last of the Bush
masks trashed.

By November we were limp
with cold and thanks,

the kind of shiver and splay
that makes a tree bend

toward its own grateful,
painful change,

believing—inside-out,
bare-limbed, entirely—

in everything. Even in winter.
Uncertain, sure, but no

longer numb with disbelief.
I thought only the future

enjoyed this kind of life:
I think I feel my limbs again.

LAURA MULLEN

Daisies

Tis sweet to know that stocks will stand
When we with Daisies lie—
That Commerce will continue—
And Trades as briskly fly—
—Emily Dickinson

Stimulus   to stem
                    then
Words
                    pluck

It's working it isn't working it's
        working it isn't
            working it's

Central   count on it
        torn

Means more answers other
Attempts on this indeterminate

Inflorescence meant a headless
Bush the white mess of ripped off

Petals "*like* or *as*" punched (2000)
Chads in the trash these

                    precincts

                    pick

Working it

may seek to reaffirm a preexisting
        belief or   court

    decision

            act out of whimsy

    isn't working it's

Growing in waste places ask not
What   but ask

                        what

Can you   gather

Working it isn't   "it is
            easy to lie there" my

Moon or dog
Days your

Golden *effeuiller le marguerite*
Our ashen air –

Waves   flower
Congressman I will think

Carefully about your proposal
And get back to you

Working it's working   *with*

it isn't   "easiest" rhizome-
Like "to lie"   for the love of

Torture

Give me your answer

                        too

ELIZABETH HUGHEY

The I Love You Bridge

day **69**

In 1964, Michelle Obama was born in Chicago. Less than one year later, the Beatles recorded the song "Michelle," which Paul McCartney wrote partially in French with the help of a friend who worked as a language teacher. Michelle Obama's mother worked at the Spiegel catalog store in Chicago. The most recent owner of that company, the Otto family, is based in Hamburg, Germany, where the Beatles got their start playing in bars in the city's St. Paul neighborhood, on the Reeperbahn, a street known as the "sinful mile." Michelle Obama grew up on Euclid Avenue. Euclid Avenue on the Southside of Chicago and Abbey Road in nearby Tinley Park are roughly 23 miles away from each other. Paul McCartney was 23 years old when he wrote "Michelle." Michelle Obama attended a high school named in honor of Whitney Young, the civil rights leader who began his career by volunteering for the National Urban League—not in Chicago, as you might expect, but in the city of St. Paul. Young left St. Paul in 1950, the year Stevie Wonder was born in Saginaw, Michigan, a city whose first European settlers were French. Stevie Wonder appeared in his first movie in 1964, the year Michelle Obama was born, and then he then went on to great fame as a singer/ songwriter. Stevie Wonder is Michelle Obama's "favorite artist of all time." Michelle Obama says that on her iPod she has every song Stevie Wonder has ever recorded. In 1982, Stevie Wonder and Paul McCartney recorded the duet "Ebony and Ivory," which became the most popular pop song ever about racial harmony. That same year, Michelle Obama started her freshmen year at Princeton, where she would eventually challenge the college's methodology for teaching French because she thought it should be more conversational, that the words they learned should go together well. Years later, on Michelle Obama's first date with Barack Obama, they went to see Spike Lee's *Do the Right Thing*, a film that opens with the Public Enemy song "Fight the Power," the first line of which was taken from a speech given by Thomas N. Todd, an eloquent attorney and civil rights activist who lives on the South Side of Chicago. The song was later released on Public Enemy's celebrated third album, *Fear of a Black Planet*, which the group's front man Chuck D has compared to the Beatles's celebrated album *Rubber*

Soul, which was, of course, the album on which the song "Michelle" appeared. When Paul McCartney first played "Michelle" in the studio, John Lennon suggested that he add a bridge between verses. The night before, John Lennon had listened to a recording of "I Put a Spell on You" by Nina Simone, the singer/songwriter and civil rights activist who moved to France in 1992, the year Michelle and Barack Obama married. John Lennon loved the way that, in her version of "I Put a Spell on You," Nina Simone sang, "I love you. I love you. I love you," and so Paul McCartney added a similar line to "Michelle." Speaking of love, one of Barack Obama's favorite songs is "Sinnerman," the American spiritual that was made famous by Nina Simone, who released her version on the album *Pastel Blues*. *Pastel Blues* was recorded in 1965, one month before the Beatles recorded *Rubber Soul*, the album on which they released to the world the song "Michelle."

A. VAN JORDAN

"The Farmers Have Won. Not Us."

—from "The Seven Samurai" by Akira Kurosawa

At 10 am on a plane to New York, I watch
The Seven Samurai for, possibly, the seventh time.
When stories act out our greatest fears,
we never grow tired of watching others die
to prove we can go on living. Deaths on screen
make sense of the quiet defeats in our day:
the friends who forget your face, the lover
who no longer calls your name, the check
you wait for as if it were a new love,
an old friend, a new day. And this morning,
in the newspaper—like the poor farmers
speaking to the samurai in the film—
we plead to our president to save our village
from the bandits who are waiting. Like the plot
in the classic film, the bandits wait and threaten
to return next season when the crops are fuller.
As if he were a samurai, our president agrees to save us
poor farmers whose families live in fear
of what's just over the ridge of the mountains. He
collected his Ronin administration with their
distinct personalities, but even his own
economists fear what they can't see. They fear
as if they have more to lose, as if they haven't
lived through the season when the bandits
rode into the village, leaving us hungry after the harvest.
Once the bodies of the samurai fall over the crops,
their blood fertilizing our soil—
as in, once they save homes, food, children—I wonder
what last line he will utter to his surviving warriors
when he rides out of town looking over his shoulder,
as we return to work over our crops.

DARA WIER

Salmagundi Algorithm

Rain is falling all over us.
Sky-high rain, rain with a purpose.
Our petals are iffy.
Everything's iffy.
Thunder knocks hard on my head. Yours?
I worship a thoughtless weather's insistence.
Slick on the road, slick in our thoughts.
Time splintered, time buffeted.
We have drifted back into our typical orbits.
For a while we were brighter, better, drawn &
Famously happy. We forgot ourselves, surprise
Took us by surprise, we were newly minted, un-smudged,
We were scratchproof, our expiration dates so far in the future
We couldn't see them. We bounded along from hilltop to
River, from satellite to starry nights, you lent me your coat,
You gave me your shoes, you made your bed for me, you threw
Open your windows. There's always been a picture of a man dipping
His hand through the sky's liquid places. He's feeling around for escape
Portals. I see there are one or two in your eyes. I will escape through your
Eyes. If you'll let me. If you'll leave me.

I Picked Up That Strange Light Again

I'm reading in my pajamas today,
my father dying, brain swell, pneumonia.

The morning paper passes into
the world a picture of a factory

so ugly it produces only flags.
I'm reading in my pajamas today,

the crossword puzzle's a cruel joke.
The shortcuts he taught me, words

like *ale* and *ado* make all the difference.
I picked up that strange light again,

spent all night in shop windows,
coffee, tea, their reflection, the best wine

he drank at dinner, snacking up to 18 times
a day in his wheelchair. A glass of grape juice,

nurses dilute the wine. I'm reading about
Notre Dame stem-cell protestors saying life

begins at conception and they respect all religions
and all views and millions of people

who have diseases that are incurable.
When I try to talk to my friends

about flowers, I'm thinking of trees,
rifle ranges, crows. Sometimes from

the window there's nothing.
I sniff the bedclothes. Scratch my unshaved

face in the mirror. I look about as dangerous
as a guy sitting at the edge of his bed,

wishing his father beautiful visions,
hallucinations, nothing scary,

the sweet scent of morphine
the yellow leaves of honey locusts

waving in his sleep.

Onto the World Stage

day 73

We're all sure you'll rise to the occasion
though the occasion keeps sinking lower and lower.
O, aporia.

Opera, did someone say?
Not operatic but aporetic.
Even the anarchists have leaders
and even some of them, you will please.

You're here to clean up after the bullies
who people loved to pin the blame on,
yet people need someone to bully for them,
at least, to bully their bullies.
O, ballyhoo!

Let them shadowbox with the shadow banking system.

As for the bully pulpit, it's not big enough for your entourage
of 500, I read somewhere.
It's global solutions to global problems.
You can tell a basketball from a globe.
As for a global regulator, he might not.

MICHELE BATTISTE

What He Said

day **74**

The first thing I'd do, as president, is sign the
Freedom of Choice Act. That's the first thing
that I'd do.
—Barack Obama, July 17, 2007

The baby says *mama* and I
turn, kneel, offer up. The baby says
bobble and a bottle turns
up, conjured and warm. Imagine

that. The ease. The thrill. To speak
and it happens. To name and it appears.
Who other than a child wields
this power? My body is spring

-loaded with muscle, prepared
for a fight that hasn't yet
happened. Yet bearing and birthing
the child came close to breaking

my heart. The doctors hooked me
to wires, monitored the errant
blips, the horrible music
of ventricular

                    counterpoint.

Each unintentional dozing
off mimicked death's sly art.
The doctors shrugged
                  it off,
unplugged the works, wrote "benign"

in a folder and I was well.
The ease. The thrill. There will be
no more
            babies. Yet my body
insists on its rhythmic launching

115

of eggs, ignores the heart's stuttered
caution. Inside me grows
                              a tiny
fear, its flesh hard as a hollowed
-out gourd. The little shaman

chants *nu nu, nu nu nu*, calling
the milk from my breast, my breast to his
mouth. His hands clench and unclench.
His body's weight
                        on my belly.

SUSAN WHEELER

Song of the G-20 Gone

It was time for the queen to be touched so
Don't worry, Michelle, my love—
It was preordained: your touch, and
You as His shill and glove.

What would Cromwell once have made
Of your touch that drew the drape
And showed her there, that sad old gal,
Toting the box and the crepe.

It's time the queen was touched, my love,
Have no regrets, ma chère—
They carried the canary out and about,
And you were the one to dare

While, high above the city crowds,
The bankers waved their pounds,
Taunting the anarchists in the 'hood
And the stick came down upon a head,

We posed and fed, and from clear gold
Your touch turned crown to wood.
It was time for her to be held, my love,
You were merely the one who would.

MARTHA COLLINS

To Listen to Lead To

is going to listen . . . as well as to lead
listen to lead a nation the way

to lead discussion the way remarks
lead to others to something listen

lead though we say *too much too many*
the wrong not enough to listen learn

to lead us out of ourselves and into
the world its hungers angers hurts

to lead us out of a war not into
(this is prayer) another deeper

lead us not into lead us out
lead us up and on to listen

to someone listening for—

O listen to him listen

"Not a Panacea but a Critical Step"

day **77**

all the money
in the world
is not enough honor or

satisfaction. all bridges
burned a shortened life;
maybe consecrated cold—

a too-early spring
inside what buds now bloom
from spreadsheets.

up sleeves, rolled,
conservatively
kept financial records from previous

quarters, yes. the automobile
brings us burning. a slight scald
is common enough

at home,   in the workplace:
soothe beneath cold
water of diplomacy, never ice.

Rite (to Forge Armor for an Orphan)

day

for Obama, home and abroad

Let cherry blossoms amass into a thinking cap,
resilient as a helmet. Let candor be its visor.

Let mother armadillo offer her bony plates
for impervious gorget and pallettes.

Let porridge pad your ribs as inner cuirass,
and the Queen's lamb fall to furnish jambeau.

Let your elegant hand in greeting grip
with a gauntlet of persuasive valor.

From father terrapin borrow a shield;
let honor inscribe its coat of arms.

And should the glamour of stardom
reproach your enemy, let it shine, let it shine.

Let mother porcupine give quills
to stitch into a supple tuille.

Let garden arugula arise for brassart
and Swiss chard guard as sturdy cuisse.

The world is heavy freight, it shifts in transit.
Let keenness be the keeper of equilibrium.

Let sky mother bend to protect in transport
each gallant motion of your head.

Let father grass solder his longest blades
into sollerets to strengthen your steps.

Let all that thrives in air conspire to keep you safe,
and character be wrought six-fold.

So let such armor prove disarming.
Let it shine. Let it shine.

PATRICIA CARLIN

Thinking My Way Out of a Paper Bag

day

There is a tide in the affairs of men which taken
at the flood, leads on to fortune.

No more trumpet bray,
blare, scare tactics.
No more With or
Against, Black or
White.

Confusion
rains over shining seas,
flooded plains.

(O Captain. O Presidente.
We are sad,
we are scared.
We are not very pretty, most of us, and
not very rich.
Less rich now.)

Sweet country.

(Meltdown. Bears on their ice floes, rats in their bayous.)

All systems set to go.
Our little lives are rounded with an O.

CHRIS GREEN

Today

I'm holding my toddler who
is throwing up outside the pet store.
My dog is eating it
while the man next to me asks if I know
how much for the kitten in the window.
My senses heightened
to all labors, my daughter's crying
becomes a kind of loneliness so desperate
she's a sea without a boat.
At home, the care of her has the kitchen blazing.
My wife stands beautiful at the sink, wordless
but humming, dreaming of bright pink shingles.
An odd sobriety when I realize
the sexiest thing I can do is get a job,
bring news of a little money.

Elevator or Poem Written the Day after Not Showing Up for a Reading at an Embassy Official's House

I have disappointed the bureaucrats by not attending their salon.

Instead we walked lost in the stone valley with the five year old Emma feeding me imaginary food, until we ran out of vegetables.

Emma was not going to be at the salon. Her crayons are glorious flames in her tiny fists/

The email says, I guess you were confused it was the #2 guy's house, the assistant to the Ambassador, as if I was confused it was a secretary, not of State, but one who types. Perhaps if it was the typing-kind I would have attended, she would be a Macedonian woman with children at home, middle-aged and still attractive, I would touch her hand when she made a joke, there would be homemade baklava, I would help her with the dishes, there would not be servants with platters that when they walk by make me cringe.

The bureaucrats are sharpening their razors.

Paperwork.

Are you someone searching for sanctuary?

★

I am scribbling in the yellow light of this morning, I am peering out my window to count the red buses carrying the men to stand on corners and wait for work. I stir my black coffee with a fork. The rain and Arvo Part.

I am witnessing a blackbird arguing with a stray dog for a moon of bread. I am counting the gold coins to give to the man selling newspapers I cannot read but buy anyways.
I am blessing the wounds my friends carry, the ones they show me through cigarette smoke.

I am swallowing a tiny pill.

★

My old neighbor's washing machine churns through the walls telling me she is not working today.
I pass her in the elevator without a light. She was scared of me for a long time, now she utters a sound I know means hello, or goodday, or I have nothing to fear from you man in the hat pulled down above his eyes.

In the quietude of the elevator with the bulb burned out.

★

There is an embassy we all want to hide in. Or hide from?

With these last words, I throw open the doors.

CRAIG ARNOLD

Dear Steve

day **82**

you were the one today I wanted to talk to
thinking about that Tuesday last November
when everyone was happy or almost all

In New York they were happy   videos
of the hipsters in St. Mark's Place singing *oh
say can you see*   my brother wrote to say
It's pandemonium down here in Brooklyn
I was not in Brooklyn or in St. Mark's Place
but another country   and even there my friends
I saw that night were happy   the whole world
may have been happy   I hope you were happy too

I was alone careful of feeling happy
careful and cool-headed and qualified
now I am sad   it was not the time or the place
for being careful   it is the saddest thing
to stand at the edge of a crowd of people singing
and not to sing but to talk about the song
to watch and weigh and even admit a little
how singing might be good   but in the end
to feel stronger in standing silent alone

I wish I could be happy with other people
and not in spite of them   how many times
I have been invited into happiness
and held back and missed a chance to be
part of a radiance   to be transparent
to the joy of others   not always to insist
on the substance of my self   to cast a shadow
dear in its darkness only because my own

and I turn to a poet we love so much together
a city poet   a poet of reckless affections
and I hope to learn from him *to emulate*
the exhilarating life of happy crowds
and I thought that you might understand
it's not pity I need but understanding
how two people might share the sort of love
for a third thing   that they might disappear
in loving   a poet   a city   a family

so anyway   I wanted you to know
you were the one today I wanted to talk to
you were someone I could be happy
losing at last myself in singing with
no longer *everyone and I*   but *we*

KATHRINE VARNES

Some Kind of Secret Fruit

The brown women walk the pale babies around and around;
the children wear outfits more pricey than those of the women.
I smile at the women. I smile idly at the children.

First Lady Obama is planting a vegetable garden.
It may be the cameras, but I think the beds are too small.
I think about compost, how death turns around. It's Easter.

Who do you think will be weeding that garden? Let water
fall down this April; we can't afford any more root shock.
It's also Passover. I am an apartment dweller

who plants peas in her mind, watches rosemary spread.
The brown women walk the pale babies around and around.
Recession or boom, we always see circling babies.

Will busses of school children weed the White House garden?
A mother asked me to spy on her third new nanny
the day we met in the courtyard with our children.

My son (age 5) wants to tell our new president
we need labels for hot and cold milk, new boots, gloves, and a ban
on corn syrup—high fructose. Two cups trust,

one cup cash, and a half pint of exploitation?
The tomato hornworms you have to pluck off with your fingers,
then you cut them in half, leave them out for the hungry birds.

It's good to know what it is you're talking about.
My skin is the color of some kind of secret fruit.
My son said this when I asked him. I said *yes.*

CIN SALACH

The First Easter, 2009

A man flies out of Rosehill Cemetery on
his bike, singing. Did he just rise up from the grave
on two wheels? He whirls by and smiles. Jesus,

is that you? A red-haired man with a pointy beard
stands across the street. He smirks then rolls his eyes.
It is Easter Sunday. *Crazy biker guy*

his rolling eyes say. *Crazy singing biker guy*.
Last night my son kissed me for the first time and
it felt like my mouth was dipped in holy water.

He put one hand on each cheek and his open mouth
on mine. Smiled, did it again. Smiled, did it again.
Patted my shoulder and laughed as I put him to bed.

I was distracted by that love all night.
While he slept, I joined a friend on the porch
to wait for the pizza man or woman and asked

if Jesus is in the tomb right now. She is
well versed in Christianity and said *Yes,
he is meditating*. So he'll push the stone

out of the way tomorrow and walk out?
Yes, she says then adds, *This entire weekend
is about rebirth, about choosing a new way*

to be alive. A new way to do things.
You are our new way to do things. We are
84 days in to rising again.

I once thought I was secretly Jesus and
that was quite a burden. What would happen
when the world discovered? I practiced crawling

into a life-sized manger in front of our church
from a young age. My feet hung out but it was
a great fit otherwise. Do you ever want to

crawl into a cool dark place and pull the boulder
closed behind you? Or is the oval office
enough? Do you pray to your heavenly other:

Why this economy? These wars? That predecessor?
I thanked God I believed in God all the while George
W. was president. I knew that

when all was said and done, God could handle him.
Comcast news flashes up the day's headlines when
I check my email. Some mom is mad about

the White House egg roll. The girls have a new puppy
and a new name for that puppy. But I don't click
to read further. I have all the news I need.

At fourteen months my son begins to walk and
today I watch him make his way across the park,
arms out, palms up, like he is receiving

a benediction. His relationship with faith
is solid. He moves toward the slide, the swinging bridge,
big city garbage cans. All are of equal

interest. That is how I feel when I walk
in the world now. My palms are up. Open.
This is what I want to tell you.

**who is speaking—nominal
substances—who listening—anchor,
bluster, filter—to whom listen—
flattering machinations fluster the
skies—substances—from the
skies—operations fall—to be
purchased—inked into existence—
information conveyed, trucked,
stowed, migrated—on the verge of**

> *. . . perception is the brain's best guess about what is happening in
> the outside world. The mind integrates scattered, weak, rudimentary
> signals from a variety of sensory channels, information from past
> experiences, and hard-wired processes, and produces a sensory
> experience full of brain-provided color, sound, texture, and meaning
> . . . Perception is inference.*—Atul Gawande, *the* New Yorker

> *NATO's International Security Assistance Force said 'four to eight
> enemy fighters' were killed and intelligence intercepts indicated
> 'the hostile intent of the enemy to attack ISAF posts.' // . . . Haji
> Matinullah said warplanes appeared above the (Afghan) village of
> Sangar around 3 a.m. and unleashed bombs. He said four members
> of one family died, including an 8-year-old boy, and two people in
> other families were killed, including a 3-year-old girl. Sixteen people
> were wounded.*—Amir Shah, Associated Press, April 14, 2009

> *You never write what you see. You just see, and you write something
> else. There's always something else.*—Barbara Guest, *interviewed by
> Cathy Wagner*

effort   the bases   a run   win   the cycle   a president   tack

the scholar   nerves   baseball   the draft   all-stars   day   training

pitch   head   the dirt   a glance   the practice   hitch   nothing

that lesson   a quarter-century   a scholar   an interview

the president   the man   officials   insurgents   militants   the man apparatus   nations   the door   the room   the scholar   years

the king   castle   treasures   auction   jacket   organizers

items   dollars   murder   the producer   years   a sentence   a jury

murder   the producer   a host   the celebrity   murder   turf   years

the verdict   a courtroom   years   trials   police   an actress   death

a chair   mansion   a clerk   the word   mouth   the expression

proceedings   wife   years   the row   the gallery   the verdict   murder

the option   jurors   the use   a firearm   a term   years   parole   jurors

the court   trial   a jury   the verdict   a cause   rejoicing   the office

defeats   the trials   a-lister   renown   work   1970s   the pockets

the connections   cases   cases   jurors   the acquittal   the laws   cases

moment   pirates   the life   snipers   a standoff   pirates   shots

snipers   opportunities   the marksmen   position   the house

the authority   the navy   a foe   a hostage   scopes   targets   prospects

a resolution   a series   moves   the pirates   a rope   a brigand   odds

a ride   an official   deliberations   condition   anonymity   action

this case   the shot   success   details   the rescue   officials

an escalation   tactics   the coast   a surge   activity   control   limits

visits   restrictions   transfers   money   families   administration

travel   limits   transfers   money   relatives   the island   restrictions

moves   promise   advantage   winds   brother   reforms   pressure

summit   leaders   relations   government   the case   the president

momentum   change   policies   decision   a departure

administrations   tightrope   wages   allies   pay   help   governor

mayor   speech   a challenge   the tenure   a gap   the budget

the support   unions   a role   campaigns   a negotiator   the problem
the office   the steps   the city   the unions   support   the race
revenues   taxpayers   mood   wallets   workers   a slice   the increases
watch   an agreement   union   the contract   years   week   mayor
concessions   the unions   people   the workforce   the city   shortfall
light   lessons   parents   class   spirituality   classroom   teacher
hat   drawl   first- and second-graders   picnic   children   part
program   apples   the nod   offer   brownies   macaroni and cheese
eels   melons   students   something   letter   name   rules   game
reward   satisfaction   satisfaction   power   teachers   workers   jobs
star   model   index   record   nation   world   obituaries   page
protestors   demonstrators   people

BECCA KLAVER

I Didn't Buy It

With head cocked and one eyebrow arched
for a while there I was very uncool for my age
My Friends My BFFAEs My Top 8 My Faves
weren't colorblind or post-nothin'—bolder
they meant to reassign values to the spectrum
as only pissed and earnest heirs can, lit up by
fiber-optic cables blinking across the night—
now we're on the grid, now we're on the grid
—Gen 2.0 e-moans   wonders if it was a trick
to get them to Home Depot to buy mops and
then update their status and then drive home
buy Home Depot stock and update their status

    Me, I saw a politician who pleased the senses
    And I was earnest and pissed and wrong, too

JOHN GALLAHER

There Are Many Theories
about What Happened

The bright yellow newspaper stand is selling papers
where the president is waving. It's April.

We stood a little off to one side. "We're
watching the president for a hundred days," we said.

The president on a plane. The president
playing basketball.

"Was there enough about the drapes? The puppy?"
we asked all winter.

"At different times of the day,
the president appears older or more luminous,"
we said. However old we got. However old
we started.

It's day 87, and our trees are looking like real trees
in bright green, almost yellow,
so that the still town looks like a real town.

Maybe the body really is you. Maybe a picture
is a fact.

And our river is looking like a real river, with a dock,
and a boy and his father fishing.

There's a picture of the president with a dog.

We want so many things.

Letter to a Former Presidential Candidate

day

Tonight I want to write to Eileen Myles. Eileen, I want to say, do you think I should have a baby? I am forty. I ask everybody I know and even some (like you) whom I don't. I ask the Pulitzer Prize–winning poet Robert Hass in the parking lot of an Italian American deli in East Dallas. And when I pose the question I feel I am on a great ship slicing through the Atlantic. The sun cuts a rut across the ocean, a divot. Nothing seems impossible, just far away. Robert Hass says: Oh, you are trying to decide. That's difficult. We drive Robert Hass north of Dallas to Archer City. High school kids take prom pictures in front of the courthouse: boys in green Day-Glo cummerbunds, girls in spaghetti straps. Maybe it's the county seat. Robert Hass spots a scissortail flycatcher on a telephone wire. We drink sodas at the Sonic because the Dairy Queen has gone out of business. O Walter Benjamin! O Larry McMurtry! and all of your beautiful boys in the West who did not have to worry about babies!

I've been sad, I want to tell Eileen. I've been spinning around with a decision decided. A body may be finished, but the mind strains. Farid and I have $15,000 in savings, $40,000 in debt. We've seen privatizations, a loss of price cautions, a rise in sunblock. The trees know how to make more of this flat gray light across the prairie.

I grew up in suburban New Jersey. My father took the train to work in "the city." My mom had a part-time job. We spun our skateboards around the cul-de-sac, gathered at the park at dusk. We smoked cigarettes and pot. When I went to sleep, a window-box air-conditioner clicked and hummed.

Now the city won't have me. I have gone to market; I have gone on the market. I want to come to you, Eileen.

Others have offered suggestions. One poet has a chicken coop; another grows kombucha colonies in her kitchen cabinets, she wants to raise goats. Another wants to go to Maine to study the contemporary back-to-the-land movement. What do you make of our economic avant-garde? We work in state institutions; we work for private colleges; we work in offices with views of air-conditioning equipment on roofs.

Farid and I do not have time, do not have wealthy parents, no Girl Scouting skills, no collection of Foxfire books. One year we lived in a cabin on an Austin creek. A snake coiled under the sink. Day after day we hauled bags of garbage and laundry up a hillside. We were going to learn plumbing and carpentry. Instead we took our plastic rafts out onto the dirty water, watched the sun drop through the sycamore trees. The creek became a mechanism of documentation and invisibility. No one knew what nested on its banks. When the winter came, we shivered near the space heater. When squirrels crawled into the roof, we left for a duplex in Dallas, where Bonnie met Clyde, where George Oppen married Mary.

Once I asked the MacArthur award–winning poet CD Wright about children. CD Wright said: Don't worry. These days you can buy a baby on E-Bay. But if we E-bayed the baby, Eileen, we would still have to pay $7,500 a year for day care. We'd still have to find money for a down payment, replace our ten-year-old cars, plan our retirement. We are young and in love, all the movies say, we have everything. Farid says money rises as if a tall field of wheat. We will wade into it. Just beyond the window of our car on the North Dallas Tollway. No, that's corn. No, that's weeds.

Varieties of Religious Experience

day

after Fanny Howe (Day 5)

Christ yearns for the human soul.
Entire months lacked meaning.

But you wait and watch the blood build around the button-down
as glorious sweat cascades from the wicks.

Then you calmly lean forward with a hand to your face
and say something everyone agrees with.

You are grooming our premises
for fruition into a modest, literal truth.

Refreshed palette, Jesus reaching his arm through the clouds,
the air directly in front of my eyes.

Will our sufficiency really be as arbitrary
as a helicopter spotlight passing fence to fence over the suburbs?

Light spits out of my chest and peels back
the self's scaly concessions to the market.

I have suffocated under the weight of my sin, but there is hope
that my husk will arc and crumple in acceptance.

JOSHUA COREY

When I Heard the Learn'd Spokesmen

When I heard the learn'd spokesmen
Explain the contingencies that demand executive privilege,
When I read the torture memos
And heard the arguments against acts of truth
And sins of commission,
When prosecution and justice were again put out of reach in the name
    of freedom,
When I, sitting, heard the spokesmen and surrogates, to much
    applause and to much silence,
How soon unaccountable I became tired and sick,
Wandered out away from my desk and the perfections of the wedding,
Put aside residual pride and stepped into the April evening,
And once again in perfect silence, stood
And beheld the stars.

JASON SCHNEIDERMAN

Oracular

When there is mud
on the ground

you will
want boots.

When the weeds
have thorns,

you will
want gloves.

There is
much

that is
known

in
advance.

All of it
useless.

What you love,
you will rise to.

What you hate,
you will sink to.

But this is the truth
of the fool, or the logician.

Something true
that has no value.

The gods are easier
to please

than the people,
but their anger

feels
the same.

Remember: We
are not one.

Remember: We
are never each other.

When you want to see,
use a prism, not a lens.

When you want to hear,
there are many voices.

A nation is never
at one with itself.

Never.

JOY KATZ

How Poetry Saved America

In a box the size of a saxophone case
containing a brand-new 300-seat theater
serving coffee in the balcony (balcony is made of coffee lids)
and subsidized oratory.
Notice the risk managers shrunk to beads strung on a necklace of fine floss
stuck (by a thumbtack) among blinking fairy lights
signifying ~~hope change~~ luck.
A song plays when you get up close.
The soundtrack feels so good, like a full bathtub.
The experts (a bag of plastic babies)
are piled there, next to the pundits.
Their cilia move the casings of bombs (you can't see them, but—)
gently along the linings of their guts.
The framers, lead soldiers,
wear the economy in the pockets of little aprons:
green frills (tens, twenties) (really the top snipped off a bunch of dill).
The scout captains are looking in 3D (here, put on these glasses)
at how the poets made credit default swaps
into palm fronds and wove them into thumb traps.
How poetry stuck America underneath all the cakes,
lacy paper to keep things neat. (Please don't lick.)
The tall white straw stuck in the milk
signifies America went up the flagpole and mattered
and matters still.
This envelope, can you see it is the president's desk?
and this beautiful slim twig stripped of bark, our president.
Mexico is on the phone. (For each body count, a new ringtone.)
In the View-Master children sneak. Click. Across. Click.
The border. Click. They cheer.
Those aren't guns, they're sticks of gum.
Try a piece of Eager Glacier (with its warming liquid center),
Just Reward, Urban Fury. Chew a piece of Dawn Sky Song.

You say those names are from an old administration.

Oh but poetry saved them.

Water flows beneath the streets on LCDs the size of postcards.

Like them? In the gift shop.

The letter in the envelope says Mr. President, please don't give up.

ROBIN BETH SCHAER

Endangerment Finding

Admit our sun is common, a Milky Way twin
to a hundred million more. Even its end
ordinary, no stellar explosion, it will snap
hydrogen to helium then cool to a dense core.

You squint skyward, still wanting the corona
of a bright god, the unconquered sun that chose us
to spin around. But there is no need for tributes
of maize and falcon wings while we burn

the oil of light left epochs ago. You may ratify
the droughts and downpours, assign blame
for melting ice and rising seas, but I can count
more kinds of hammers than turtles;

we need instinct, not law. The dogs of Pompeii
howled for days, even snakes slithered
from Helice. In the Gallatin range, the bears
left the forest. At night, a slice of mountain shook

down, sleepers drowned in their beds, soaked
in waves off the lake. When the ground stilled
the bears returned, covered with mud. Hush.
Listen to our internal combustion rumble.

There is more elegance in turning photon
to electron to motion. Let us trade the old sun
for the new one, sustain ourselves, wet and green,
within this delicate spindle of axis and orbit.

Obama Ps (alm)

Victory begins
     with empathy
across lines
     and plummets
to retrieve
     fragments of
a nation

I beg your belief
     to summon
the unbuilt
       the unfed
the untended
     and those within
whose realm   it lies
     to rise

day 94

SEAN COLE

Freehand

My Obamaffection drooped a bit when
my best friend pointed at the drones
Baracking Pakistan. I know. I know.
You can't undo a did like the arachnid
we unleashed six years ago.
He's not Moses. And he told us
he'd do stuff we'd had enough of,
some of us. I guess I just want no
more dead anyone. Naïve I know, don't
want dead me either, will this prevent
dead me? O unflaggy heart: you don't
kvell about nations. All you want is soul
food on a boat, and music, and loose
pants to dance in during booze. Dead them
doesn't make alive me feel free. Free
child care does. (Bill O'Reilly's eyes
roll in their round graves at the sound
of this I know.) I don't want Socialism.
I want Olympus. I want a magician
to defuse the big rotator bomb we
all rent rooms in. I want my best friend to rest
no-death easy in his Mendocino tree retreat
amid mountains. O planet. Please go on
vacation. You've worked too hard at this, this
rugged disaffection that tasks granite. Your
poles are kooky durable. I wish a weird Seussian
politics on us that changes fire-throwing
ravagers into hand-holding cartoons.

Stalked by a Prisoner of Texas

You want to secede? From what? Yourself?

A prearranged harmonizing occurred
for eight long years: gun shots, obfuscations,
bleats of empowered utterance,
bombing, and presumptuous census work.

Immigrants screwed for life.

Predatory lending thrust on everyone, including poets.

Faulty few in charge of rhetoric, and now they think
all is wrong with the world.

A kind of speculative critical thought
inside a flayed fish, a lone canoe.

No utensils, everyone said.

The soul-self inside the big fat white whale.

★

It's finally a potentially remarkable world again:
intelligent discourse presented
insomuch that feats are specifically explained,
problems have reasons,
and parachutes without legitimate sense-making
drop downward in slow succession
(this interests me too).

What do you do in your spare time?
Waterboard or shoot your hunting buddy?

Some say it's too late to do something, but we know it's not.
Furthermore, there's something going on here: a quasi-romantic
    sentiment
likening white men to endangered animals.

The wreck of the self transformed into an awkward, odd mightiness.

day **97**

Market Storm

Why shouldn't I bubble and boom?
My underbelly torques whole horizons
touched by the many-mortgaged, the risers high.

Also, my altostratus, low
rolling, keeps coming back, proving
cedars in the red, sun leak, worse. Wealth

withdraws. And just what codswallop
got you here? Didn't I surrender my capital,
my privately owned focus? I still have my same

to-do list, the laundry and dry cleaning,
my outlays and interests, the kerfluffle
of debts, paid and un- and how

long did I let the much-rubbed money bristle
over your old assembly lines, model T's,
silicon valleys, canneries for peach? Once

upon a time, a man said, *I believe.*
Dear Sir, dear key in the lock, who says
your house can't be the house by which it stands,

saying, *book, pitcher, cupboard, gun
unloaded on a high shelf?* Pray to me right:
aim cloud bank, brave storm, see index,

trust public, pay attention, take downpour,
read invisible hand, blast tumult of billions.
Rub the coin, take me in, dress the wound.

Guilt Armada

(draft of a haibun)

About a hundred days into the dream, I saw a ship. I feel free to hide it
here. A poet can hide anything in her poem. Some think this exceptional
freedom is why we are at war. How can presidents sleep? Do they take
pills? I feel free to ask. They give orders to kill people they don't know.
This president is an intelligent man; he's like a son. The top of my left
hip—where the femur meets the pelvis—feels turquoise. Arthritis or
something. The president has compromised his ideals. How does he sleep
after sending soldiers for endless violent occupations since Gandhi is on
his list of top ten. Give him time, say my friends. Even now he looks tired.
He does not say "endless violent occupations" but I am free to say it. I can
choose Grande or Tall, Blackwater, oil & opium. The handsome general
sits in the Appropriations Hearing. Nice haircut. His medals look like the
little colored bands they put on pigeons. He has talked two presidents
into endless violent occupations. Do presidents get stoned on power or
what. Give him time, say my friends. Even the people crouching in the
Shadow Banks & changing their shadows in shadowy corners say Give
him time. Tossing their used-up shadows in the sea.

> The outline of a ship came
> & then the ship
>
> It sailed right up my hip

The good war, already a billion dollars every two days & they ask for 83
billion more. Burger & a tallboy, Blackwater, oil, opium. Not that we don't
need opium. We definitely do. I need some for my left hip right now—for
the turquoise. I could have ended up like Coleridge had I used opium but
I am allergic. Opiate products say Please Please Please & I say No. Please?
No. My heart stopped on a hospital gurney because of an opiate product &
the orderly shouted CODE BLUE. It was like America, that stopped heart.
People could get up from their computers & protest the torture & profits of
military contractors but their hearts have stopped.

> with what was never done
> what was never made

Many poets have ships in their bodies: Baudelaire, Rimbaud and Mallarmé, not to mention Homer. Give us time, says the president, look forward. Why do you keep saying that. Didn't they teach you to use your rear-view mirror when you learned to drive? Look behind or you might back up over the neighbor's cat. I don't feel like looking forward. I want my heart not to stop again. I want to look back at the women crouching in their houses. At the row of small fires on the beach.

> ancestors waved & cried
> *Put this in the guilt armada*
> *Not a regatta we're an armada*
>
> under the burning moon
> the burning sky

JENNY BROWNE

24 Hour Roman
Reconstruction Project

To hold both masking tape and scissors,
glue stick and pen labeled permanent?
Does this poem need a branch of myrtle in it?

Lately, I've been tracing the flight paths
of a dollar bill then cutting it
into halves and I have knots. Could you

rub a bit harder, and to the left, please?
The invitation says you don't need to bring
your own weapon. You can make one

when you get here. In Texas we've got
an ammunition shortage and a cute
mixed-race point guard trash-talking

the Mavericks' center. Do you know him?
Don't shoot the mistake.
Don't shoot the doctor in the face.

Yes, there will be wrestling.
Yes, there will be snacks.
When the immortal skyline proves mutable.

When a child is born three weeks (we say) early
and by this mean the difference between
expectation and crowning.

My fellow shillabers, my tired Visgoth,
late it gets. Time lapse makes
a flower bloom so fast.

First Grade, All Over Again

day **100**

[1]

When he was little
and just a boy
and called Barry,

his report cards
were shown, first,
to the one person

whose approval
mattered the most,
his mother, Ann Dunham.

Works well with others
who do not work
well with each other.

Another GOP *No*,
another honor roll of polls,
locked-in telephoto.

[2]

Barry Obama was
African-American,
African father, American mother,

but not Barack,
Barack Obama is mixed,
race-less and Black.

I have seen more photos
of Barack Obama
than I've ever seen

of my own mother.
Blame the Press,
digital photography, all

the camera-phones,
raised like Rockefellers,
above the rest of us.

[3]

My mother hates
being aimed at. "But Mom, this is
a really good camera,

a Leica." So what, it's
all German to her
and that means torture,

already half locked-up
with my brother.
Armed robbery, his war crime.

My parents broke up
the day Jimmy Carter
was inaugurated,

the last time swine
sent to wipe out drug cartels
came home to roost.

[4]

There's no way to stay
"on-subject" and do this
without high marks

for marksmanship.
Some bald class bully
taking shots at him,

saying he's not tough.
Saying he's a brown Apologist,
shaking hands with

future allies-of-color
weakens us, so let's waterboard Bo,
the biracial Water Dog.

Let's let the human eye decide
if color-blind is cultural
or regular-blindness.

[5]

Mother's Day in the White House,
Marian and Michelle.
First Granny and First Lady.

Out of vernacular-respect,
Black men often refer
to the women they love as "Mama."

This is not something
the minority expects the majority
to accept, reconciliation.

"Once a man loses his mother,
he can accomplish
damn-near anything."

I heard this on the streets
of Washington, D.C.,
right outside the office of citizen.

Biographies and Process Notes

Elizabeth Alexander (Washington, D.C.) is the author of several books, including *American Sublime*, which was a finalist for the Pulitzer Prize, *Antebellum Dream Book*, and *The Venus Hottentot*. Her awards include a National Endowment for the Arts Fellowship and a Guggenheim Fellowship; she currently teaches in the Department of African American Studies at Yale University. She wrote and read the inaugural poem "Praise Song for the Day" at Barack Obama's swearing-in ceremony; the poem has been published by Graywolf Press and is reprinted here.

"My job was to address the occasion in some way but also hopefully do it in language that would have resonance beyond the occasion. My challenge also was to do it with the utmost clarity, but clarity that did not sacrifice complexity. And I told myself, 'OK, the hard work is the making of the poem. When you read it, you're sort of setting it free.'"

Kazim Ali (Oberlin, Ohio) is the author of two books of poetry, *The Far Mosque* and *The Fortieth Day*, and two novels. A book of lyric prose essays, *Bright Felon: Autobiography and Cities*, will be published fall 2009. He teaches at Oberlin College and is a founding editor of Nightboat Books.

"I believe that compassion for humans must come from the understanding of the vulnerability and tenderness of the individual human body. In the years since September 11 I came to understand my own body and its existence in space through the words 'random search,' through my separation from other bodies, the hands that moved across it. At some moment I chose not to pack a book with Arabic script in my carry-on bag. It's not only me who was 'dehumanized' by the experiences. My poem 'Random Search' started as a note of forgiveness to the countless workers who subjected me to indignity; it ends instead as a prayer of hope."

Nin Andrews (Poland, Ohio) grew up on a farm in Virginia. She is the author of several books, including *The Book of Orgasms* and *Sleeping with Houdini*; her next book, *Southern Comfort*, is forthcoming. She is the recipient of Ohio Arts Council grants. And she wants you to know that Poland, Ohio, went for Obama.

"When I wrote 'Hoi Polloi' I was thinking about the confusion Americans feel about questions of culture, class, race, education, religion, etc., and I was thinking about how Obama himself has been accused of being too elitist and too ordinary, too rich and too poor, Christian and Muslim, black and not really black, a celebrity and a mere community organizer."

Craig Arnold's second book of poems is *Made Flesh*; his first book, *Shells*, won the Yale Series of Younger Poets Prize in 1999. He taught at the University of Wyoming, and spent spring 2009 in Japan on a U.S.-Japan Creative Artists Residency exploring volcanoes.

Sally Ball (Scottsdale, Arizona) is the author of *Annus Mirabilis*. She's the associate director of Four Way Books and teaches at Arizona State University in Tempe.

> "I live in a neighborhood where there have been a lot of foreclosures, a lot of burst-bubble-bad-news. People are either in bitter flight or else they can't get out, which sits on them whether or not they actually want to go anywhere. It's McCain's home state. There seemed to be a kind of meanness in the air in March: a local bumper sticker reads, 'How's all that hope and change working out for you?' The (loose) villanelle form was a way to tamp down a poem that was written in one chaotic day, in airports and planes, en route from Tampa to Tempe (the jumbly names of those cities seemed to endorse the formal decision—small substitution, serious shift)."

Catherine Barnett (New York, New York) is the recipient of a Guggenheim Fellowship, a Whiting Writers' Award, and a Pushcart, and the author of *Into Perfect Spheres Such Holes Are Pierced*. She teaches at Barnard, the New School, and NYU. She also works as an independent editor and recently collaborated with the composer Richard Einhorn on the libretto for *The Origin*, his multimedia oratorio about the life of Charles Darwin.

> "In the weeks before Obama was elected, I began saving the *New York Times* in a tidy stack; I continued until the inauguration, as if this small private act of 'preserving' the 'truth' would help keep Obama safe enough to get to the podium. By January 20, the stack of papers probably reached my shoulders. I placed them in a big cardboard box so that I would have proof, a record, of these miraculous months; I knew I couldn't comprehend it all as it was unfolding. Once I received Rachel and Arielle's invitation, I began more purposefully reading the paper every day, trying to use the day's news in my poems. I was surprised by the appearance of the literal news—the material news—in this tiny poem."

Michele Battiste's (Astoria, New York) first full-length collection, *Ink for an Odd Cartography*, is forthcoming, as is her next book, *Slow the Appetite Down*. She's currently at work on a book-length narrative series of poems about post-WWII Budapest. She teaches for Gotham Writers' Workshop and raises funds for Helen Keller International, a global health organization. She lives in Queens with her husband and son.

"I was absentmindedly listening to public radio, and my ears pricked up when the reporter mentioned that a senior Vatican official stated that if Obama signed the Freedom of Choice Act (FOCA) 'it would be the equivalent of a war.' I thought, 'This is a war I'm ready for,' and went to work on my first maneuver. I went to my primary source, the body, and found what I needed to arm myself."

Jeanne Marie Beaumont (New York, New York) lives in Manhattan and teaches at the 92nd Street Y and in the Stonecoast MFA Program. She is also director of the annual Frost Place Advanced Poetry Seminar. Her books are *Curious Conduct* and *Placebo Effects*.

"Since Obama was traveling overseas, I was thinking about how many in our country and the world regard him somewhat as a 'knight in shining armor,' restoring honor to government. Yet I've also heard expressed over and over immense concern, even anxiety, for his safety. So I thought to create a fanciful coat of protective armor, using several details in the news at the time."

John Beer's (Chicago, Illinois) poems and prose have appeared in numerous outlets, including *Barrow Street*, *Denver Quarterly*, and *Xantippe*. He studies philosophy and social thought at the University of Chicago and reviews theater for *Time Out*.

"Walter Benjamin writes of Franz Kafka: 'One is tempted to say: Once he was certain of eventual failure, everything worked out for him en route as if in a dream.' This, in a nutshell, is my process in general; the only extra ingredient in writing 'My Calamine Lotion' was telling it like it is."

Erin Belieu (Tallahassee, Florida) is the author of three poetry collections. Her most recent book, *Black Box*, was a finalist for the *Los Angeles Times* Book Prize. Belieu teaches in the Florida State University Creative Writing Program in Tallahassee (a.k.a. The Scene of the Crime) and she wept tears of joy when Florida went blue.

"At the time my poem was due for this project, the elation many of us felt at President Obama's election was starting to ebb, to be replaced with a collective realization of 'Sweet Jesus. Things really are a gigantic mess.' In my poem I was trying to suggest a kind of comic intimacy around this inevitable and necessary moment."

Marvin Bell's (Iowa City, Iowa, and Port Townsend, Washington) book *Mars Being Red* appeared in 2007. His latest book is a collaboration, *7 Poets, 4 Days, 1 Book*, coauthored with the poets István László Géher (Hungary), Ksenia Golubovich (Russia), Simone Inguanez (Malta), Christopher Merrill,

Tomaž Šalamun (Slovenia), and Dean Young. His two sons are, among other things, a country music singer-songwriter with a strong sociopolitical bent and a trained ninja who helped guard the Dalai Lama in New York City.

"I liked the timing, the sense of community, and the sociopolitical nature of this project and, also, the variety it proposed. I wrote my piece very late at night."

Mark Bibbins (Brooklyn, New York) is the author of two collections of poems; *The Dance of No Hard Feelings* and the Lambda Award–winning *Sky Lounge*. He teaches in the graduate writing programs at the New School, where he cofounded *LIT* magazine, and Columbia University.

"The poem describes the circumstances of its composition in a way that I almost always avoid, but I was following Erin Belieu's cue and 'letting my freak flag fly' (see Day 23). It's a good thing that a) I don't get my news from television and b) McCain/Palin didn't 'win,' because I'd have to trade in my freak flag for a straitjacket."

Susan Briante (East Dallas, Texas) is the author of *Pioneers in the Study of Motion*. She is an assistant professor at the University of Texas at Dallas. She lives in East Dallas with the poet Farid Matuk.

"I wanted to write about our economic crisis using a new set of terms. I also wanted to pay homage to the sense of intimacy one gets from listening to the president and the first lady. It's a strange intimacy we feel as fans of public figures, whether they are politicians or poets. It seems false and comforting all at once."

Jenny Browne (San Antonio, Texas) is the author of *The Second Reason* and *At Once*. She lives in downtown San Antonio and teaches creative writing at Trinity University. The title of this poem, as well as a few of its lines, comes from a project by artist Liz Glynn in which a group of volunteers realizes the entire architectural history of Rome, in cardboard, in a day.

"Day 99 felt both full of potential and primed for doom, like doing all your shopping at midnight on Christmas Eve. What world could one possibly save and/or ruin in a single day? A *New York Times* article about an artist who created and then smashed a detailed cardboard replica of Rome gave me a starting point. Then, as I was drafting the poem, editor Arielle Greenberg's son arrived, surprising both her and the poem with his early emergence. Indeed, everything can change in a day."

Laynie Browne (Tucson, Arizona) is the author of seven collections of poetry, most recently *The Scented Fox*, winner of the National Poetry Series. She currently teaches at the Poetry Center at the University of Arizona, where she is developing a new program to bring poetry to public schools.

"I very much admire poets who write occasional pieces but have not written many myself. I scanned the daily news, looked into the mystical associations of the number '44' (for our 44th president), and also tried to write an epistolary piece. In the end this small 'ps (alm)' seemed best to capture the historical moment and the admiration and hope Obama inspires."

Linda Buckmaster (Belfast, Maine) is the current poet laureate of Belfast. She has published three chapbooks of poetry: *AfterLife, Momentitos, A Mexican Journey*, and *Heart Song & Other Legacies*, which took second place in the Maine Writers and Publishers Alliance competition's self-published category. Her poetry, fiction, and journalism have appeared in numerous journals. She is adjunct faculty in communication in the University of Maine system, and her "day job" is with Women, Work, and Community.

"I don't usually write haiku, but this topic and the emotion attached to it seemed so big that I played with the simple form to distill my thoughts. I started with the traditional seasonal reference—March in Maine and maple sugar season—to capture the waiting, hope, potential, and energy attached to this change in administrations."

Patricia Carlin's (New York, New York) new book of poems is *Quantum Jitters*; her previous collection was *Original Green*. She teaches literature and poetry writing at the New School in New York City. She coedits the poetry journal *Barrow Street* and Barrow Street Books.

"I had planned to write a collage poem made up of fragments from newspapers, magazines, and internet postings appearing within three days of my assigned date. I wanted fragments and multiple voices because I felt no one voice would catch my often contradictory moods and thoughts about the national situation and Obama himself, to say nothing of the complicated external reality that seemed to shift minute by minute. I was put off, though, by the deadening repetitive language of the reporting, whatever the source. And I realized that to make these fragments speak as I wanted would take a lot of space. I went in the other direction, experimenting with using mood shifts and different language registers within a very small space. I also wanted to use a lot of 'O' sounds at the end, knowing I wanted them all to resolve in the final skewed Shakespeare quote."

Sean Cole's (Arlington, Massachusetts) poems have appeared in various magazines including *Black Clock, Pavement Saw*, and *Dad*. He's also published a chapbook called *Itty City* and a full-length book of postcard poems, *The December Project*. He's a reporter for public radio, a Bay Stater, and a trigenarian.

"The way this wracked my nerves, you'd think I had to write the inaugural poem itself. Four false starts. I was quaking that at least ninety-nine other poets who'd truly aced the assignment were going to be reading this poem. I don't tend to write a lot of political poetry. As a reporter, I try to stay nonpartisan in public. Plus I was concerned that the poem would read as too critical of the president at this transitional and historic time when he needs all of our support. A test was the reading I did in Wendell, Massachusetts, a few days after I wrote the poem. There was dead silence in the room as I read the first few lines. But when I was finished, a voice in the back of the room called out: 'Yeah, man!'"

Martha Collins (Cambridge, Massachusetts) is the author of the book-length poem *Blue Front*, which won an Anisfield-Wolf Award, as well as four earlier collections of poems, two collections of cotranslations of Vietnamese poetry, and two chapbooks. She is editor-at-large for *FIELD* magazine and an editor for the Oberlin College Press.

"When I wrote my poem, President Obama had left the G-20 Summit in London and gone on to France. But I remembered something White House Press Secretary Robert Gibbs had said the week before: that the president was 'going to listen in London, as well as to lead.'"

Nicole Cooley (Glen Ridge, New Jersey) grew up in New Orleans. Her third book of poems, *Breach*, about Hurricane Katrina and its aftermath, will be published next spring. She directs the new MFA Program in Creative Writing and Literary Translation at Queens College–City University of New York and lives outside of New York with her husband and two young daughters.

"This poem was written as part of my ongoing, now lifelong effort to keep the people of New Orleans, my native city, from being forgotten. And it was written in the spirit of Muriel Rukeyser who wrote, 'What three things can never be done? / Forget. Keep Silent. Stand alone.'"

Joshua Corey (Evanston, Illinois) is the author of two full-length books, *Selah* and *Fourier Series*, and two chapbooks. He teaches English at Lake Forest College and lives in Evanston, Illinois with his wife Emily and their daughter Sadie Gray.

"This poem's current form is partly the product of a misunderstanding on my part: I had somehow persuaded myself that it was due on Sunday, April 19, when in fact that was the day it was scheduled to be posted. So there I was on Saturday night, enjoying my cousin Rachel's wedding, when my phone buzzed with a polite e-mail from Rachel Zucker to remind me that my poem was due at midnight! Fortunately, I had written a draft of the poem that was basically ready to go; unfortunately, it was on my computer at home. Between a rock and a hard place, and assisted by champagne, I reconstructed the poem right there on my phone and sent it in with an hour or two to spare. I have this experience to thank for the phrase 'perfections of the wedding,' which refers to the literal occasion but also, in the context of my Whitman homage, becomes a nice metaphor for my ambivalence about the affectionate embrace in which I and eighty-one percent of Americans now grip Barack Obama—in spite of my numerous reservations about his middle-of-the-road policies."

Patrick Culliton's (Chicago, Illinois) poems have appeared, or will soon appear, in *Coconut, Conduit, Third Coast*, and elsewhere. He is the recipient of a 2009 Individual Artists Fellowship from the Illinois Arts Council. He teaches at the University of Illinois–Chicago.

"Confession: I wrote most of this poem, texting it into my phone on a CTA bus, a few weeks before my due date. When I transcribed it from my phone a few days later I thought, 'This might work.' I did force myself to reenter, adding to the poem as my day approached, so as not to feel like a total cheater. That it's a 'personal' poem, and its rhythm, are both nods to Frank O'Hara, my favorite president. I also felt it fitting to submit a personal poem in the wake of such an impersonal administration."

Mark Doty's (East Hampton, New York) most recent book of poems, *Fire to Fire: New & Selected Poems*, won the National Book Award for Poetry. This fall he joins the faculty at Rutgers University in New Brunswick, New Jersey.

"My poem was written on the day before its appearance online, when it seemed the only word in the news was 'money,' and there was no subject but debt. Economics is such a befuddling subject that I'd usually avoid trying to write about it except in some very particularized way, but I stumbled across a brilliant half line from Thomas McGrath's 'Letter to an Imaginary Friend,' and then I was off."

Sean Thomas Dougherty (Skopje, Macedonia) is the author or editor of eleven books, including the forthcoming *Sasha Sings the Laundry on the Line*, *Broken Hallelujahs*, and the novella *The Blue City*. He is currently on tour as a Fulbright Lecturer, reading across the Balkans, and teaching at Cyril Methodius University. This summer he and his family will be returning to the United States and complete and utter unemployment.

"I witnessed each unfolding day of the Obama project as an expatriate, a position that always made me hyperaware of myself as an American in a manner I wouldn't be back home. This changed the position of my poem's speaker, who, though happy with the administration, still feels the need to point out the inequities of power that reside wherever Americans wander, and the true place of poetry, which is wherever there is an open door."

Michael Dumanis (Cleveland, Ohio) is the author of *My Soviet Union*, winner of the 2006 Juniper Prize for Poetry. He is an assistant professor of English at Cleveland State University and the director of the Cleveland State University Poetry Center.

"One week before the 2000 election, I fell in love with (and started to date) a brilliant and beautiful woman. The first time she cried in my presence, and I cried in hers, was when the media preliminarily called Florida for George W. Bush. The next few years proved rough for both of us, both personally and politically. A lot of horrible things happened. We waited, Samuel Beckett–style, for a conclusion to the Bush years, as though the end of them would lead to a much happier time in our own lives. We almost made it. We last spoke on the day Obama picked Joe Biden as his running mate.

"This poem I tried to write about Obama was a challenge. It wasn't easy to begin, to find an angle. I felt too jaded by the past to be too jubilant about the present. His election and inauguration felt too recent for me to be able to say anything meaningful. However, I had quite a bit to say about George Bush, now that he was no longer on television, and about the relationship that failed to outlast his presidency. Sitting down to write, I exclaimed in frustration, 'I have nothing to say about the new president!' That's how this poem happened."

Cornelius Eady's (South Bend, Indiana) latest book of poems, *Hardheaded Weather*, was nominated for a 2008 NAACP Image Award. He is cofounder of Cave Canem and teaches at the University of Notre Dame.

"In Elizabeth Alexander, Obama selected the one poet I felt had the poise and mother wit to represent the new generation of African American poets. 'Praise for the Inaugural Poet' is my attempt to reply to her 'Praise Song for the Day.' What I saw and heard that inaugural afternoon was an African American poet reading a poem that somehow was public and interior, somehow old and new. And brave enough to risk the word 'love.' My hope is that one day, folks will rewind it to see just how good that moment was. She took a breath, then off she sailed."

Thomas Sayers Ellis (Brooklyn, New York) is a photographer and poet and the author of *The Maverick Room*, which won the John C. Zacharis First Book Award, and a recipient of a Whiting Writers' Award. He is a contributing writer for *Waxpoetics* and *Poets & Writers*. He is also an assistant professor of writing at Sarah Lawrence College and a faculty member of the Lesley University Low-Residency MFA Program, and he contributes TSE's Pick of the Week at www.tmottgogo.com.

"I wanted to pay homage to the work of mothers and their effect on this current example of change. I wanted to do this lightly while suggesting the cyclic nature of learning, gaining approval and being tested, both personally and professionally. President Obama's journey from Barack to Barry back to Barack is not an uncommon identity trajectory. It rings of liberation struggle and changing song, from soft to hard, not the opposite."

Jeff Encke's (Tukwila, Washington) poetry has been published in the *American Poetry Review*, *Fence*, and *Quarterly West*, among others. In 2004, he published *Most Wanted: A Gamble in Verse*, a deck of playing cards featuring excerpts of love poems written to Saddam Hussein and other war criminals. He holds a doctorate in English from Columbia University and currently teaches literature at Richard Hugo House in Seattle.

"I settled on the subject of water-boarding after several abortive attempts, which included one poem about army ants in the voice of Marlin Perkins and another entitled 'Rush Limbaugh, Queen of the GOP, Eats an Avocado.' It was a rough weekend."

Jenny Factor (San Marino, California) is the author of *Unraveling at the Name* and serves on the Core Faculty in Poetry in the MFA Program at Antioch University, Los Angeles. The opening lines in her poem echo medieval poet Sa'adi's *Gulistan* (1258 A.D.), which were quoted by President Obama in his recent Nowruz greeting to the Iranian people.

"I'd been struck by a KCET documentary on Depression-era photographers, including Dorothea Lange and Rod Stryker, commissioned by FDR through the New Deal to document the needs of farmworkers as he traveled the country. Obama had just visited Los Angeles, touching down at the Pomona Fairgrounds. He was stumping for a new economic plan that would encourage American self-expression through labor. Congress was already chiseling away at the stimulus package, excising the movie industry, the arts, sports sponsorships. I listened to Obama's Nowruz greeting. I sat down for twenty minutes every evening for the five nights leading up to my day and I put down some words in any shape. On Day 55, Kazim Ali's couplets reminded me of a ghazal. Day 58, Carmen Giménez Smith made me aware of the risks of the word 'hope.' On Day 62, Arielle Greenberg's poems in storefront windows seemed like an art act similar to Lange's photographs. The couplets in a ghazal are supposed to be like detachable beads from a necklace. So all day long on my day, I worked at each pair of lines, until I heard the bead in them clink."

Betsy Fagin (Brooklyn, New York) is the author of the chapbooks *Belief Opportunity*, *Rosemary Stretch*, and *For every solution there is a problem*, as well as a number of self-published chapbooks. After living abroad for four years, she got back to Brooklyn just in time to vote.

"Day 77 occurred during the G-20 Summit. Combined impressions of the summit, auto industry bailout, and a welcome return to diplomacy inform the poem."

Ann Fisher-Wirth's (Oxford, Massachusetts) third book of poems, *Carta Marina*, has just been published. Her chapbook *Slide Shows* is forthcoming, and she is coediting, with Laura-Gray Street, an international ecopoetry anthology, *Earth's Body*, which will be published in 2011. Ann teaches poetry and environmental studies at the University of Mississippi. She and her husband have five grown children.

"My husband and I spent a year in Sweden in 2002–2003, as the United States under George Bush was preparing inexorably to invade Iraq. Following the escalation from overseas and seeing firsthand how passionately the rest of the world opposed U.S. policy were instructive and deeply traumatic. Then, last fall, I worked to register voters here in Mississippi—and met people I will remember always. My poem is for them."

Katie Ford (Philadelphia, Pennsylvania) is the author of *Deposition* and *Colosseum*, which was named a Best Book of 2008 by *Publishers Weekly* and among the Top Ten Poetry Books of 2008 by the *Virginia Quarterly*. She is a recipient of a 2008 Lannan Literary Award.

"I wrote this poem as a kind of extension of my poems in the first section of *Colosseum*, but this time with President Obama in office. There are 'found' pieces in this poem, which are quotations taken from George W. Bush, 911 calls, and a CNN correspondent reporting during the first night of the flood of New Orleans."

Todd Fredson's (Shelton, Washington) poems have appeared in *Blackbird*, *Puerto del Sol*, *Poetry International*, and other journals. He received his MFA from Arizona State University in 2007. He directs the nonprofit McReavy House Museum of Hood Canal and works as a writer and researcher at Read Right Systems in Shelton, Washington. He lives with his wife and their two sons in the Skokomish Valley.

"'Air and Simple Gifts' was performed at Barack Obama's inauguration by Yo-Yo Ma and Itzhak Perlman. It is based on Aaron Copland's 'Simple Gifts,' which was composed around an old Shaker hymn. At the swearing in of Dwight Eisenhower in 1953, Copland was banned from playing a scheduled composition of a piece called 'Lincoln's Portrait' because an Illinois congressman complained of Copland's liberal politics. I remember the radio commentator saying quietly that Bush's term had just expired when

Perlman and Ma were in the middle of this piece. The piece stuck with me, and its tone guided the observations and impressions that I gathered until the few days before writing my poem."

John Gallaher (Maryville, Missouri) is the author of three books of poems, most recently *The Little Book of Guesses* (2007) and *Map of the Folded World* (2009), and an online chapbook, *Guidebook* (2009). He lives in rural Missouri and coedits the *Laurel Review*.

"I didn't have any plans for the poem leading up to the day I was to send it, though I did read the blog daily and write a couple practice poems for earlier days, which gave me a tone to work with. In the end, the poem I wrote came from looking at newspapers the day I had to write the poem. The title comes from David Brooks' editorial in the *New York Times*. The rest from just looking around a bit. The first family's new dog. My little town in the Midwest. And then the hypothetical Midwest."

Chris Green (Evanston, Illinois) is the author of *The Sky over Walgreens* and *Conceptual Animals*. He recently edited the anthology *A Writers' Congress: Chicago Poets on Barack Obama's Inauguration*. He is a visiting fellow at DePaul University's Humanities Center. He lives in Evanston, Illinois, with twin daughters and a very nice wife.

"For me, the challenge of this project was the waiting for Day 80, the thinking without writing. It was a strange game of planning to be spontaneous. My plan was to make the political personal. Luckily, once you have kids, everything is personal, and almost every moment a potential poem. 'Today' came quickly, but not easily—it started as another poem about another moment, but as poems often do, it grew into something new."

Arielle Greenberg (Belfast, Maine, and Evanston, Illinois) is the author of *My Kafka Century* and *Given* and coeditor of the anthologies *Women Poets on Mentorship: Efforts and Affections* with Rachel Zucker and the forthcoming *Gurlesque* with Lara Glenum. She's an associate professor at Columbia College Chicago and on the faculty of the Stonecoast MFA Program. She is currently living in Maine and working on two nonfiction projects: a guide to choosing to birth with midwives and a book about back-to-the-landers. Her third child was born at home on Day 96 of this project.

"Launching this project, and writing this poem, both of which felt like perhaps the most 'public' poetry work I've ever done, coincided with the very inward 'nesting' state of the third trimester of pregnancy for me. I was aware of feeling more cut off from and disinterested in the Outside World (whatever that is), and also more connected to it, than when I am not about to have a baby. So I struggled with how to be honest about that selfish, survivalist state while trying to engage in what was going on outside of my uterus and my family. When I watched a city council meeting on cable access one night, I knew this would be my path into a poem: the way the micro and local connect up with the national and global; the way intimate choices about, say, shopping and cooking and birthing are interwoven with enormous, planetary concerns."

Ian Harris lives with his wife and son in Portland, Oregon. His work has been published in the *Black Warrior Review*, the *Kenyon Review*, and *AGNI*.

"I was never that jazzed about Don Henley's ode to expired summer love, 'The Boys of Summer,' until March '09, as the new presidential guard was settling in and the economy was crumbling. Henley captures that end-of-summer, fin-de-siècle feeling so well and—for a moment—the song seemed an eerie soundtrack to the last of the good times. I wrote the poem under Henley's spell."

Brenda Hillman's (Kensington, California) eighth collection of poetry, *Practical Water*, will be published in 2009. With Patricia Dienstfrey, she coedited *The Grand Permission: New Writings on Poetics and Motherhood*. She is the Olivia C. Filippi Professor of Poetry at Saint Mary's College in the San Francisco Bay area and works with CodePink, a women-initiated grassroots peace and social justice movement.

"Lately, I've been trying to address the named emotions. Guilt (and the gilt within it) is a feature of daily life, yet it remains mysterious and brings news. This particular Guilt Armada sailed from 'emergency supplemental war funding' discussions in the Appropriations Committee last week (after Obama had said the Congress should not use that particular method of continuing to fund these wars). Petraeus had just said he thought it would be necessary to send more National Guard troops. The structure of the haibun form and the journal/verse combination is appealing to work with: in traditional haibun, there are strict haiku for the verse passages, but I like to take liberties. I had just been teaching a prose poetry section in my prosody class a few weeks before."

Jen Hofer (Los Angeles, California) is a poet, translator, interpreter, teacher, knitter, and urban cyclist. Her recent and forthcoming poem sequences, collaborations, and translations are available through a range of autonomous small presses, including Atelos, Counterpath Press, and Ponzipo. She also makes small books by hand at her kitchen table in Cypress Park. Her most recent work consists of antiwar-manifesto poems that explore the languages of power and information mediation.

"This text is a translation of the front page of the *Los Angeles Times* from April 14, 2009, and was written on April 14, 2009."

Fanny Howe (La Jolla, California, and West Tisbury, Massachusetts) is the author of more than twenty-five books, most recently *The Lyrics*. Her book of essays, *The Winter Sun: Notes on a Vocation*, is forthcoming.

"The poem was already partially written when the 100 days were about to begin. Since the poem was already in the political realm, it seemed to be poised to jump in line, once I had worked on the words some more."

Elizabeth Hughey (Montague, Massachusetts) is the author of *Sunday Houses the Sunday House*. She grew up in Birmingham, Alabama, and now lives in Massachusetts with her husband and son.

"On my day, I had planned to read the newspaper to get my head in the right space for the spirit of this project. However, I started talking to my husband about the song 'Michelle,' and we got carried away finding links between the song and the Obamas. I kept thinking I'd turn back and write the poem I'd planned to write, but I was having so much fun with 'The I Love You Bridge' that I just had to finish it and send it to Arielle and Rachel."

Major Jackson (New York, New York) is the author of two collections of poetry, *Hoops* and *Leaving Saturn*. He is an associate professor at the University of Vermont and a core faculty member of the Bennington Writing Seminars. He serves as the poetry editor of the *Harvard Review*.

"Writing the poem for this project felt like writing an occasional poem, and there is nothing better than rhyme to hitch your cause célèbre. I waited until Day 22, my assigned date. That morning, en route to Santa Fe for a Lannan Foundation event, I read a host of online, mainstream newspapers such as the *New York Times* and the *Washington Post*, and a few liberal websites, such as the Huffington Post, in airport terminals at LaGuardia and Dallas/Fort Worth, occasionally glancing up at the ubiquitous CNN broadcast on the flatscreen. The top news: bank executives were on Capitol Hill attempting to convince the nation to bail them out, and Obama was flying Airforce One to Elkhart, Indiana, to announce and sell his economic 'stimulus package' to America. So both Obama and I were on the road. Of course, I was selling a clinically proven, extremely effective and safe product for boosting the economy: poetry! (Specifically, Walt Whitman's poetry.) Maybe it was too easy, but I made a formal leap into the sexually ambiguous dimensions of the expression 'stimulus package' as a means of discussing the seductive and rhetorical qualities of both politics and language."

Patricia Spears Jones (Brooklyn, New York), an African American poet and playwright, is the author of two collections, *Femme du Monde* and *The Weather That Kills*. Mabou Mines commissioned and produced *Mother* (1994) and *Song for New York: What Women Do When Men Sit Knitting* (2007). Coeditor of the groundbreaking women's poetry anthology *Ordinary Women: New York City Women Poets* and contributing editor to *BOMB* and *Heliotrope* magazines, she is originally from Arkansas and has lived in New York City for over half her life.

"How do we make a more perfect, stronger Union? We knit together a stronger Whole. So I used the Fates, as each sister has some measure of a person's life. I also used the self-destruction of the would-be Niagara Falls suicide and the Alabama murderer to provide real world unraveling in the poem. I wanted to make a poem that asked all of us to forgive our self-destruction and start to make a better nation, a healthier world."

A. Van Jordan (Ann Arbor, Michigan) is the author of *Rise*, which won the PEN/ Oakland Josephine Miles Award and was selected for the Book of the Month Club by the Academy of American Poets. His second book, *M-A-C-N-O-L-I-A*, was awarded an Anisfield-Wolf Award and listed as one of the Best Books of 2005 by the *London Times* (*TLS*). *Quantum Lyrics* was published in July 2007. Jordan was awarded a Whiting Writers' Award and a Pushcart Prize, and he is a recipient of a John Simon Guggenheim Fellowship and a United States Artist Williams Fellowship. He is a professor in the Department of English at the University of Michigan.

"I wrote this poem, at the suggestion of the editors, the night before it was due. I spent the weeks leading up to it reading the Huffington Post and the *New York Times* very closely. In airports around the country, I would also catch snatches of CNN. Watching *The Seven Samurai* again, I felt that Obama's job would be as thankless and herculean as the job of the poor samurai in the film."

Allison Joseph (Carbondale, Illinois) teaches at Southern Illinois University– Carbondale and is the author of five books of poems.

"The poem came from reading Meghan McCain's column in the *Daily Beast*. So many attacked her for saying she couldn't find a decent date after her father's defeat in November, but I felt for her. She holds an uneasy position in this day and age—young, conservative, but not anti-gay (loved it when she called the Republican Party on its use of homophobia). Meghan's a young woman to be admired, even if Laura Ingraham and Ann Coulter resort to name-calling about Meghan's figure."

Joy Katz (Brooklyn, New York) is the author, most recently, of *The Garden Room* and is editor-at-large for *Pleiades*. She teaches poetry workshops at the New School and NYU and lives in Brooklyn with her husband and young son.

"I'm a slow writer. The last poem I finished, before this one, is about a photograph of a lynching. The image haunted and haunted me; I threw out hundreds of drafts over eight years (I remember starting the poem at the beginning of George W.'s first term in office). When I finally said to myself, 'Who am I to write about this?' I realized that was the subject of the poem. With the 100 days assignment, I felt similarly humbled—as George Oppen said, poetry can't do anything 'for a people'—yet I felt challenged to write something big. Something titled either 'How Poetry Saved America' or 'How Poetry Failed America.' I carried these two titles around in my head as the weeks passed, during which time the economy grew more and more bleak. As my assigned day approached, I realized poetry can save America, if you think of 'save' not so much as salvation but as safekeeping, keepsaking, mythmaking. I am both delighted by and deeply suspicious of a poet's ability to transform and distort events through language. In that way, poetry isn't so different from the news. But it's a lot more fun."

Paul Killebrew (New Orleans, Louisiana) was born and raised in Nashville, Tennessee. Last September he moved to Louisiana to work as a lawyer at Innocence Project New Orleans. His first book, *Flowers*, will be published this year.

"On Day 5, I read Fanny Howe's 'Imagine All the People,' printed it out, and taped it to my bedroom door. On Day 85, I wrote a pale imitation of it."

Geraldine Kim (San Francisco, California) was born in 1983. She is the author of *Povel* and of the play *Donning Cheadle*. She is currently working on her next book, which doesn't have a title yet. It features zombies and robots and an unnameable sadness. She plays electric violin in the band, Two Boobies and a Vagina."

"After realizing that the poem I originally submitted wasn't going to format correctly, I wrote this one in two hours—writing whatever came to my mind, even sounds—and vacillating between my feeling of childish hope and cynical doom for Obama's administration."

Becca Klaver (Chicago, Illinois) is the author of the chapbook *Inside a Red Corvette: A 90s Mix Tape*, a founding editor of the feminist poetry press Switchback Books, and the assistant programs director of literature and poetry at Columbia College Chicago. She starts her PhD in literatures in English at Rutgers University in fall 2009.

"People my age graduated from high school the spring of the Columbine

Massacre, were in college on September 11, 2001, have seen the war in Iraq drag on and on, and now are starting careers (or exiting them due to lay-offs) in the midst of a recession. After growing up in the seemingly carefree 90s, we're trying to grapple with the world in which we've become adults. If not for Obama and his rousing calls for hope, my generation might not feel motivated to help clean up; on the other hand, that hope coexists with indignation over the mess we've been handed. Like the words 'earnest' and 'pissed' in the poem, these feelings sit side by side, almost rhyming but ultimately irreconcilable."

Caroline Klocksiem (Northport, Alabama) grew up in Columbia, South Carolina, and recently moved to Tuscaloosa, Alabama. She is a Massachusetts Cultural Council Fellow and poetry coeditor for the online journal *42opus*, with poems most recently published or forthcoming from *Slurve*, *Hotel Amerika*, and *Drunken Boat*.

"I wrote this thinking mainly of these two things: 1) the notion of do-overs that strikes me as particularly American, and my hope that the new administration will manage to repair some damages from the last; and 2) My solidarity with and allegiance to regular, non-CEO folks, like the workers at my grocery store and my enlisted buddies and their families."

Wayne Koestenbaum (New York, New York) has published twelve books of poetry, criticism, and fiction, including most recently *Hotel Theory*. He is a Distinguished Professor of English at the CUNY Graduate Center and currently a visiting professor in the painting department of the Yale School of Art.

"I'd planned to write a more public and hortatory poem—more point-edly 'political'—but then I came down with the flu and all I could think about was my body."

Katy Lederer (Brooklyn, New York) is the author of the poetry collections *The Heaven-Sent Leaf* and *Winter Sex* and the memoir *Poker Face: A Girlhood among Gamblers*, which *Publishers Weekly* included on its list of the Best Non-fiction Books of the Year and *Esquire Magazine* named one of its Best Books of the Year. Educated at the University of California at Berkeley and the Iowa Writers' Workshop, she serves as a poetry editor of *Fence Magazine*.

"This poem is based on an executive coaching session I underwent while working in a corporate environment in midtown Manhattan. I was intrigued by both the purity and porousness of the language employed by the coach—it was so antipoetic it became poetic. Obama's language—and the language of Washington apparatchiks generally—strikes me as similarly 'pure' and multivalent at once."

David Lehman (New York, New York) is the author of several collections of poems, including *When a Woman Loves a Man* and *Jim and Dave Defeat the Masked Man* (with James Cummins). He is series editor of *The Best American Poetry*, which he initiated in 1988, and is the editor of *The Oxford Book of American Poetry*.

"I had been reading Abraham Lincoln's poem 'My Childhood Home Revisited,' which begins conventionally enough but turns movingly into a lament for a childhood friend who had lost his reason. In my sonnet, I lifted images and phrases from Lincoln's poem. Who is 'the Sad tall guilty mute / giant'? I'm not saying, but the 'stains / of blood' on the portal instruct the Angel of Death kindly to pass over this house."

Amy Lemmon (Astoria, New York) is the author of the poetry collections *Fine Motor* and *Saint Nobody*. She is an associate professor of English at New York's Fashion Institute of Technology and lives in Queens with her son Bobby and her daughter Stella, who was diagnosed at birth with Down's syndrome. March 21 has been designated World Down's Syndrome Day.

"I requested my day because I'd been wondering about the new administration's commitment to supporting people with disabilities and their families. I wanted to write about my daughter. The acrostic form gave me a comfortable framework, with the phrase 'HOPING FOR CHANGE' running down the page; Stella's school picture–proofs provided a triggering image; and I finished the poem as my niece was reading one of Kipling's 'Just-So Stories' to Stella and her little cousin."

Lyn Lifshin (Vienna, Virginia) has published more than 120 books, most recently *Persephone*, *Another Woman Who Looks Like Me*, and *The Licorice Daughter: My Year with Ruffian*. She has also edited four anthologies.

"My poem came out of the sense of something new and green and exciting as the tulips in the poem."

Cate Marvin (Staten Island, New York) is the author of two books of poems, *World's Tallest Disaster* and *Fragment of the Head of a Queen*. She is an associate professor of creative writing at the College of Staten Island, City University of New York. She lives in the only New York City borough that, alas, did not go to Obama.

"On February 8, several articles detailed how our government was attempting to relieve these banks of their 'bad assets.' It struck me as ridiculous that banks would receive assistance for unwise investments. I considered the fact that banks and credit card agencies have never been particularly sympathetic to me when I've made poor financial decisions. The realization that banks were really screwing the American (and international) economy reminded me of Pound's *Cantos*. While most people consider the *Cantos* the ravings of a madman, it seems he may have had a point. So when I began the poem, I tried to pull in a few lines directly from the *Cantos* as a sort of homage to Pound. (A couple of these lines remain. I'll leave the task of identifying them to the reader.)"

Joyelle McSweeney (Mishawaka, Indiana) is a cofounder and editor of Action Books and *Action, Yes*, a press and Web quarterly for international writing and hybrid forms. She is the author of the novels *Flet* and *Nylund, the Sarcographer*, as well as *The Red Bird* and *The Commandrine and Other Poems*. She teaches in the MFA program at Notre Dame. She wrote this poem on Wednesday, February 18, 2009, and completed it at 10:54 A.M.

"I wanted to write a poem for this site that would turn away from domestic politics, or even American foreign policy, and operate from another position. On my particular day, preparations were being completed for the trial of Khmer Rouge member Comrade Duch at the Hague. Comrade Duch, formerly the schoolteacher Kaing Guek Eav, headed the Tuol Sleng prison complex and oversaw the imprisonment, torture, and death of thousands of his countrymen between 1975 and 1979. But my poem is not 'about' this. The poem tries to operate on some axis of powerlessness and power, with retribution and the desire to exercise justice or just be a species of (specious?) power."

Erika Meitner's (Blacksburg, Virginia) first book, *Inventory at the All-Night Drugstore*, was published in 2003. She teaches in the MFA Program at Virginia Tech.

"We live in a new housing development in a tract house that we affectionately call a 'McNugget,' as it's too small to be a McMansion. Our developer shut down development on the rest of the plots surrounding our house due to the economy and the nonexistent housing market, so we have a ton of idled machinery around here, and my two-year-old son loves to yell out names when we drive past them: Backhoe! Digger! Dump truck! I'd been listening to a lot of NPR in the car too (a habit left over from the election), and whenever my son heard Obama on the radio he'd say, 'O-mama,' so I thought these things together might make a poem."

Michael Morse (Provincetown, Massachusetts) is a 2008–2009 Fellow at the Fine Arts Work Center and teaches at the Ethical Culture Fieldston School in New York City. He has published poems in *A Public Space*, *Ploughshares*, and *Tin House*. He is thrilled—despite the socioeconomic mess (e.g., A.I.G.) that our president has inherited—that Obama is our point guard.

"I was thinking about a James Longenbach essay ('An Examination of the Poet in Time of War') discussing poetry, social climate, and whether poems need to deliberately address the occasions that spur us to speech. I wanted to juxtapose the idea of a poem's immediate occasion (lower case: Obama's attending a Bulls-Wizards NBA game) with the broader, big-picture chaos (all caps, bold face: our economic and social mess as exemplified by A.I.G.) that Obama has inherited from years of regulatory oversight. I've always thought the market-as-game analogy to be both appropriate and unfortunate, something that the winter's revelations of Ponzi schemes and odd bonuses brought home."

Laura Mullen (Baton Rouge, Louisiana) is a professor at Louisiana State University and the author of five books, including *Murmur*, *Subject*, and *After I Was Dead*. She is a frequent visitor at the Summer Writing Program at Naropa. Jason Eckardt's setting of "The Distance (This)," from *Subject*, premiered at the Miller Theater in New York and was performed at the Musica Nova Festival in Helsinki in February.

"I stay loosely attuned to news, but this project tightened my attention as it increased my sense of responsibility. It's very unusual for a contemporary American poet to be *expected* to say something political, and I loved the challenge of stepping into that space. And the poem is (in part) about expectations: not only the extraordinary pressure on a particular president or a specific policy, but also the yes/no of hoping for life-affirming change while acknowledging limitations and life-destroying errors. I also want to say that the blog felt like part of a general blooming of a space to think, feel, and speak in—and that that freedom, after eight years of dull silence, is wonderful!"

Lesléa Newman (Northampton, Massachusetts), the poet laureate of Northampton from 2008 to 2010, has received poetry fellowships from the National Endowment for the Arts and the Massachusetts Artists Foundation. Her fifty-seven books include the poetry collection *Nobody's Mother*, the short story collection *A Letter to Harvey Milk*, and the children's book *Heather Has Two Mommies*.

"The idea for the poem came to me relatively easily, as I began writing it very shortly after Inauguration Day, which meant that the image of the president and the first lady dancing together was still fresh in my mind. The concept of 'firsts' as in the first night, the first African American president, the first lady, and the first dance suggested the technique of repetition to me. And then, a dozen drafts later, the poem was done."

Aimee Nezhukumatathil (Fredonia, New York) is the author of *Miracle Fruit* and *At the Drive-In Volcano*. She is an associate professor of English at SUNY–Fredonia and lives in western New York with her husband and son.

"Having Obama elected means so much for our natural resources on this earth, which coincidentally are often the very life source of my writing. I wrote this to give words to the fauna and foliage that cannot speak, but who are surely rejoicing that we elected someone who pledges to protect them."

Mendi Lewis Obadike's (New York, New York) book *Armor and Flesh* won the Naomi Long Madgett Prize. With her husband Keith Obadike, she composed *The Sour Thunder*, an Internet opera, and curated Crosstalk: American Speech Music. Their opera-masquerade *Four Electric Ghosts* opened at the Kitchen in May 2009. She is a Cotsen Postdoctoral Fellow in race and ethnicity at Princeton University.

"I was thrilled to participate in this project and enjoyed the challenge of engaging with the realm of governmental politics in a timely manner. I chose the form of a parable because at the time I was working on a folktale and it seemed like a complementary form. And, too, what's better than a parable?"

John Paul O'Connor's (New York, New York, and Franklin, New York) poems have been published in the *Indiana Review*, *Lilies and Cannonballs*, and *Rattle*, on whose website you can hear him read his poem "Stone City." He hopes we will all do what Obama has urged us to do, which is to keep the pressure on to make sure he is the president we want him to be.

"I'm skeptical of presidential power because I know what sort of deals need to be made and what sort of contracts must be forged to be elected to high office in a hypercapitalist country such as ours. Still, it was impossible not to be swept up with the astounding fact that the home of the KKK had elected a black president, especially in the wake of the past eight years of dismal politics. I tried to include details of my daily life and interior life in this poem, which concerns my beliefs about change and the amazing times we suddenly find ourselves in. Part of my interior life included the contemplation of the horrible and continuing news of the war crimes in Central Africa, for which the Western world cannot escape responsibility."

Kevin Prufer's (Warrenburg, Missouri) newest books are *National Anthem*, which was named one of the Best Five Poetry Books of the Year by *Publishers Weekly*, and *Fallen from a Chariot*. He's also editor, with Wayne Miller, of *New European Poets* and *Pleiades: A Journal of New Writing*.

"I had a hard time getting the bad taste of the Bush administration out of my mouth when I wrote my poem just five weeks after Obama's inauguration. The result was several false starts and, finally, a poem that seems to me to dwell as much on the troubled landscape Bush left behind as any joy about Obama's election."

David Roderick's (Greensboro, North Carolina) was the 2007 Amy Lowell Traveling Scholar; his first book, *Blue Colonial*, won the *APR*/Honickman Prize. He teaches in the MFA Program for Creative Writing at the University of North Carolina, Greensboro.

"I'd never written an angry poem before, let alone a deliberately political one, but during the week of my '100 days' assignment I was troubled by some disturbing circumstances surrounding President Obama's presidency. I recall that a man was arrested for carrying a gun onto White House property and that there were news reports about the rising membership of white supremacist groups. Even closer to home, I overheard men in the locker room at my gym making some startlingly racist remarks. I found it difficult to write a poem in such a compressed time frame, and my effort here was born out of anger, frustration, and fear rather than the excitement I feel for Obama and his presidency."

Matthew Rohrer (Brooklyn, New York) is the author of several books, including *A Hummock in the Malookas*, which won the 1994 National Poetry Series Open Competition, *A Green Light*, which was shortlisted for the 2005 Griffin International Poetry Prize, and *Rise Up*. With Joshua Beckman he wrote *Nice Hat. Thanks* and recorded the audio CD "Adventures While Preaching the Gospel of Beauty." He hss appeared on NPR's All Things Considered and The Next Big Thing, has been awarded the Avery Hopwood Prize and a Pushcart Prize, and has been widely anthologized. A chapbook-length action-adventure poem, *They All Seemed Asleep*, was recently published. He teaches in the creative writing program at NYU and lives in Brooklyn.

"On inauguration day I was walking down the street with my daughter and the sun came through the clouds and I'd had a lot of coffee and somehow my spirit lifted, and I thought it might actually work. When Rachel and Arielle contacted me about the blog project I wrote this poem in five minutes and didn't change a word. I like the attention you have to pay to the rhythm when you use exactly five words per line, and the uncertainty."

cin salach (Chicago, Illinois), the author of *Looking for a Soft Place to Land*, has collaborated with musicians, painters, video artists, dancers, and photographers in such groups as the Loofah Method, Betty's Mouth, and ten tongues, with whom she recorded the CD *A Wide Arc*. She lives in Chicago with her partner Chris and her son Leo and is quite happy as a stay-at-home-mom who writes short poems during long naps.

"I am a big fan of rules (following them and not) and took seriously the 'not writing until the day before your day' part of the assignment. Listening to the world extra hard the day the poem was to be written woke up new/old poet body parts that were fed by this project."

Lisa Samuels (Auckland, New Zealand) is an American in New Zealand, teaching at the University of Auckland. Her new and forthcoming poetry books are *The Invention of Culture*, *Throe*, and *Tomorrowland*, and her current projects include *Metropolis*, a fantasy of urbanization.

"I wondered how it might feel to be in the mind and body of Barack Obama waking up on Sunday morning to his family and responsibilities. While hovering in a tender feeling toward him, I imagined being him at breakfast, and I tried to write his interior consciousness as interlaced with policy and news fragments."

Elizabeth Scanlon (Philadelphia, Pennsylvania) was born in Washington, D.C., and currently lives in the nation's first capital. She is an editor of the *American Poetry Review*.

"My son was undergoing a series of developmental tests around the time that I wrote this, and so these ideas about idiosyncratic use of language and perception of social cues affected my reading of everything in the news and gave me a heightened awareness of who-says-what. Obama continues to thrill me with how well he speaks."

Robin Beth Schaer (New York, New York) is the recipient of fellowships from the Saltonstall Foundation and the Virginia Center for the Creative Arts. Her work has appeared in the *Denver Quarterly*, *Barrow Street*, and *Washington Square*, among other journals, and recordings of her poems are featured on the website From the Fishouse. She lives in New York City and works at the Academy of American Poets.

"Writing a poem in the midst of an experience, with the clock ticking, was both terrifying and exhilarating. Being a single voice mixed with a chorus of ninety-nine others, each responding to these hundred days, offered a potent reminder of the ability of poetry, in both writing and reading, to provide (and demand) the most sublime consideration and transformation of a moment."

Jason Schneiderman (Brooklyn, New York) is the author of *Sublimation Point*. His poems and essays have appeared in numerous anthologies and journals including *Best American Poetry*, *Tin House*, and *The Penguin Book of the Son-*

net. He has received fellowships from the Bread Loaf Writers' Conference, Yaddo, and the Fine Arts Work Center. The recipient of the Emily Dickinson Award from the Poetry Society of America, he is currently completing his doctorate at the Graduate Center of CUNY.

"I wanted to get at that space between the individual and the group— that little frisson where our love of rugged individualism meets our love of the division of labor. I don't know how to be part of a corporate body, but none of us has the option of leaving."

Prageeta Sharma (Missoula, Montana) is the author of three poetry collections: *Infamous Landscapes*, *The Opening Question*, and *Bliss To Fill*. She is an associate professor of English and the director of the Creative Writing Program at the University of Montana–Missoula.

"My poem came out of a morning ritual of reading the news online while checking my e-mail. My personal e-mail account and spam folder contain the usual bombardment of listserv e-mails and elaborate and/or insular subject headings. The appearance of these various e-mails, I think, can be objectively amusing—all the listservs with funny or strange subject headings, all filtered into one e-mail box. So that day I wrote the poem stolen from one of the curious subject headings in my inbox. I thought it would be funny to add 'from Texas'—that week, there were many discussions about Texas voting for succession—and then started to enjoy thinking about Texas as a kind of character."

Brenda Shaughnessy (Brooklyn, New York) is the author of *Interior with Sudden Joy* and *Human Dark with Sugar*, winner of the 2007 James Laughlin Award and finalist for the 2008 National Book Critic's Circle Award. She is the poetry editor of *Tin House* magazine and is currently a lecturer in poetry at Princeton University.

"I had considered myself an optimist, or at least a 'things will get better' kind of person. I had not realized the extent to which my faith, hope, and feelings about being an American had completely atrophied during the long Bush era. When Obama was elected, I was not only thrilled and excited and overjoyed but surprised—phantom limbs (faith, hope, and my identity as a citizen) had grown back! It was a miracle, but then—like the trees springing to life each year–it was just a change that had been a long time coming."

Martha Silano (Seattle, Washington) is the author of two books of poetry, *Blue Positive* and *What the Truth Tastes Like*. She teaches at Bellevue College in Bellevue, Washington.

"When he won, we turned down the TV, cranked up Cocoa Tea's 'Barack Obama,' and started dancing. Two days later we were still dancing. That's when I got the e-mail from Rachel that it was time for me to write this poem."

Carmen Giménez Smith (Las Cruces, New Mexico) is an assistant professor of creative writing at New Mexico State, publisher of Noemi Press, and editor-in-chief of *Puerto del Sol*. Her book *Odalisque in Pieces* will be published in 2009.

"I wrote this with the mood of familiarity in mind that was fostered by Obama supporters in Las Cruces and across the country. I had also been thinking about the 80s and how this administration signals to this Gen-Xer the end of some absurdities we've lived with for some time."

Patricia Smith (Tarrytown, New York) is the author of five books of poetry, including *Blood Dazzler*, chronicling the tragedy of Hurricane Katrina, which was a finalist for the 2008 National Book Award and one of NPR's Top Five Books of 2008, and *Teahouse of the Almighty*, a National Poetry Series selection. She is on the faculty of the Stonecoast MFA Program at the University of Southern Maine.

"A few days after the election, I was on the subway, with one other African American person at the other end of the car. When he met my eye, he simply mouthed the name 'Obama' silently, and we smiled at each other. I was intrigued by the way that word became such a huge language, meaning so much beyond the mere sound of it. I treasured that quiet communion and began to think of how many times, how many ways, it was being repeated around the country. When I sat down to write about it, I decided to replace that nodding silence with chaos."

Laurel Snyder (Decatur, Georgia) is the author of *The Myth of the Simple Machines*, *Daphne & Jim: A choose-your-own-adventure-biography-in-verse*, and a bunch of books for children. But mostly, she's a mom.

"My challenge was avoiding skepticism. If the country could be truly earnest and hopeful, I wanted to avoid doubt myself, and look openly ahead. For me, Ahead + America = Highway."

BJ Soloy (Des Moines, Iowa), who moved from Chicago to Iowa just in time to caucus for Barack Obama, has recently had some work published in *Court Green*, *27s4evah*, and *DIAGRAM*. He works at an animal hospital and lives with the poet Julie Rouse and their hound, Mr. Dr. Solomon Von Chickenpie.

"The word 'transition' abounds re: a new administration and is used as part of such sensationalist, always updating coverage. It reminds me how temporary an experience is, even when precontextualized as 'historic,' how it's cast against other unstable memories for definition, and how it's steered by an idea of a particular future, which, if it's a desirable one, could be a definition for 'hope.' So I found a scrapped stanza in an old journal, moved it into the present, and guessed it into the future. This whole parade of lines, days, administrations, etc., met, we can hope, with attention, empathy, and scrutiny."

Leah Souffrant (Brooklyn, New York) was awarded a New York Foundation for the Arts Fellowship in Poetry in 2007. Souffrant is cochair of the Poetics Program at the Graduate Center, CUNY, where she is a PhD candidate. She teaches literature at Baruch College and writes in Brooklyn, where she lives with her husband and daughter.

"I felt deeply moved by the election of Obama and wanted to capture some of the measured optimism that was coursing about in the early weeks and months of his presidency. The reality of suffering and the gentle persistence of hope in spite of it were in my mind while thinking about writing the poem. My date, March 12, was a bloody day in the tabloids: random acts of violence, shooting sprees. I also did a bit of research on this date in history, which appeared at the conclusion of the online version as the following: 'Post Script: A hundred years ago: Lunch. Little. Epidemic. Breaks and cuts. Bad news. Women vote in Copenhagen! Gangsters pursued! Gangsters! War ships to Nicaragua! I don't know much of anything. I just don't know, crystal ball, online oracle, memory. On that March 12, people were dying. Plague, smallpox, rats. And people were born.' I wanted the poem to be about the day and date, to be as timely as possible while still acknowledging a history of thought and action, a human tradition of that tension between pain and hope."

Sasha Steensen (Fort Collins, Colorado) is the author of several books, including *A Magic Book*, *The Method*, and *The Future of an Illusion*. She teaches creative writing and literature courses at Colorado State University, where she also coedits Bonfire Press and serves as a poetry editor for the *Colorado Review*.

"On my allotted day, Day 9, I taught two classes; oversaw a thesis defense; gave an introduction to a reading; fed and diapered my two-year-old; and had blood drawn to monitor my pregnancy-related platelet problem. All the while, I listened to the news and jotted down any words or phrases that occurred to me as a response, and after putting my toddler to bed, I returned to my raw material to produce 'Wintry Weather and Job Slaughter,' a poem that takes its title from two prominent news headlines of the day."

Cole Swensen's (Iowa City, Iowa, and Washington, D.C.) most recent book is *Ours*. She is the coeditor, with David St. John, of the anthology *American Hybrid*. She teaches at the Iowa Writers' Workshop.

"Despite being surrounded by people constantly, despite having the adoration of at least half the world, Obama, I think, is very alone in facing his challenges. He has a unique relationship to them, a one-to-one relationship, in a way."

Brian Teare (San Francisco, California) is the recipient of Stegner, National Endowment for the Arts, and MacDowell Colony poetry fellowships. He is the author of *The Room Where I Was Born* and *Sight Map*; his third book, *Pleasure*, is forthcoming in 2010. He lives, teaches, and makes books by hand in San Francisco.

"'Citizen Strophes (Oakland)' came together this way: the occasion made me dive back into the journals I kept during the last three years of the Bush administration. The tremendous longing for connection U.S. citizens have brought to bear on Obama's election threw into stark relief the effect of those last years with Bush. With the question, 'What did a citizen feel like in those years?' as my guide, I found myself using the journals to collage together a poem focused on those moments in Oakland when citizenship had been so thwarted that connection between fellow citizens felt fraught, impossible, or downright dangerous. I suppose I wanted Obama to remember that a lot of healing is necessary for this country that has, in wounding others, wounded itself so deeply."

Craig Morgan Teicher's (Brooklyn, New York) first book, *Brenda Is in the Room and Other Poems*, won the 2007 Colorado Prize for Poetry, selected by Paul Hoover. A book of fiction and fables, *Cradle Book*, will be published in 2010. Poems are forthcoming in *The Best American Poetry 2009*. He lives in Brooklyn with his wife and son.

"First, I must confess I was unable to adhere to the 'day of' rule—I just can't come up with a poem so quickly. But that gave me a chance to think about the larger issues around the change in leadership that were nagging me: coming of age as a poet during a time when public discourse was so debased, when a presidential address had the value of a toothpaste ad, made me nervous about what language was capable of. It's deeply reassuring to now have a president who seems to know how powerful—and dangerous—a word can be."

Yvette Thomas (Chicago, Illinois) was born about twenty-eight years ago in Cleveland. She now lives in Chicago and will graduate with a MFA from Columbia College in 2009. She has published poems in *27 rue de fleures* and *elimae*, and is currently working on a chapbook.

"This poem was composed while walking the streets of the Windy City."

Mónica de la Torre (Brooklyn, New York) is author of two books of poems in

English: *Talk Shows* and, most recently, *Public Domain*. She was born and raised in Mexico City, where her Spanish book of poems *Acúfenos* was published. She is senior editor of *BOMB* magazine.

"I knew that if I spent enough time listening to talk radio and reading the newspaper throughout the day, by the evening my mind would have processed information in a way that would bring my point of view into focus. I was fortunate: my poem was due on the second day of Obama's first trip to Europe as president. Some of the debates on the U.S.'s role abroad started sounding as skewed as the old ones I grew up with south of the Mexican border. Those who blamed everything on American grandstanding now wanted the U.S. to solve the mess that the world economy was in. O binaries, is there nothing but evil empire or superhero in our depleted imaginations?"

Tony Trigilio (Chicago, Illinois) is the author of *The Lama's English Lessons*, several chapbooks, and two books of criticism. With Tim Prchal, he coedited *Visions and Divisions: American Immigration Literature, 1870–1930*. He teaches at Columbia College Chicago, where he directs the Program in Creative Writing–Poetry and coedits the poetry journal *Court Green*.

"As I worked on the poem, I found myself coming back to the protest over President Obama's commencement speech at Notre Dame. My father's health took a steep decline that same week, and the poem slowly began to take the shape of a goodbye to my dad. I finished it a few hours after he died."

Pimone Triplett's (Seattle, Washington) third collection of poems, *Rumor*, is due out fall 2009. She is also the author of *The Price of Light* and *Ruining the Picture*, as well as coeditor of *Poet's Work, Poet's Play*. She is an associate professor in the Creative Writing Program at the University of Washington.

"I knew I wanted to employ some 'economic' vocabulary, and when I got the notion of capitalism itself starting to talk up a 'storm,' it seemed like a good countermeasure for tone and stance against the more technical language (though the latter somehow decreased as I continued). Also, the collective call for an economic 'turn' pushed a literal turn into the poem, a shift in consciousness from complaint into the imperative mode."

Sarah Vap (Shelton, Washington) is the author of *Dummy Fire*, which won the 2006 Saturnalia Poetry Prize, and *American Spikenard*, which won the 2006 Iowa Poetry Prize. Her next book, *Faulkner's Rosary*, is forthcoming in 2010. She is coeditor of poetry for the online journal *42 Opus* and lives with her husband and their two sons on the Olympic Peninsula.

"The morning I wrote this, I remembered that space is shaped like a saddle. This, and my thoughts of Obama, merged into some kind of twisting reflection of our real-time superfast Obama mythmaking . . . Atlas, Sisyphus, Jesus, King David, the magi, magician, shaman . . . Who is he??"

Kathrine Varnes (Larchmont, New York) was born in Germany on the day after President Kennedy was assassinated and now, after many moves, may be settling in Larchmont, where she writes prose and verse while raising her son. She has published a book of poems, *The Paragon*, seen her play *Listen* produced, and coedited, with Annie Finch, the handbook and anthology *An Exaltation of Forms*.

"After eight years of living in the Midwest and South, I was happy to return to the East Coast shortly before Mr. Obama became President Obama. How lucky that I was assigned the day before Easter, when I felt the loss of my Missouri garden the most, and was pressed to develop a larger sense of what it means to garden."

Catherine Wagner's (Oxford, Ohio) latest book, *My New Job*, is forthcoming. Her other books are *Macular Hole* and *Miss America* and several chapbooks. She teaches at Miami University in Ohio.

"Some headlines on March 10 were about job losses and Obama's plans to ramp up the U.S. presence in Afghanistan, and I was looking at a picture I had just hung in my living room, a not-very-good (but effortful and beautiful and bright yellow) painting by my grandmother, who was young during the Depression—a rural scene, with a figure repairing a fence. Good luck, I thought."

Diane Wald (Dedham, Massachusetts) has been writing seriously since JFK was in office; before that, not so seriously. She works for animal welfare and lives in Massachusetts with her husband, the writer/photographer P. Carey Reid. They share their home, Spoonrest, with five fine cats. Look for *The Yellow Hotel*, *Lucid Suitcase*, and *faustinetta, gegenschein, trapunto*.

"I was very happy to participate in this project. Even though I'm not at all in the habit of writing on a 'topic,' Obama's whole candidacy and election meant a great deal to me. It pulled me out of decades of bitterness about politics. I suppose that's why I had to write about smiles."

Anne Waldman (Boulder, Colorado, and New York, New York) is the cofounder of the Poetry Project at St. Mark's Church and the Jack Kerouac School of Disembodied Poetics with Allen Ginsberg at Naropa University, where she currently serves as artistic director of its Summer Writing Program. She is the author of over forty books of poetry, including *Marriage: A Sentence*, *Fast Speaking Woman*, and the Iovis trilogy; *Manatee/Humanity* will be published in 2009.

"The poem is an amalgam of various streams related to my sense of

President Obama the particular day I wrote it. It was composed 'on the road' during a reading tour. I had been visiting sights in Illinois related to Abraham Lincoln as well as Native American ritual mounds."

Lindsey Wallace (New York, New York) is about to be a first-year MFA student in poetry at the University of Montana–Missoula. She is a two-time recipient of the Nettleton/Hirsch Prize for Poetry. Her work recently appeared in *Words and Images*.

"After attempting to book an online flight multiple times and encountering the same 'system error' message each time, the text of the error message stuck in my head as a sort of frustrated meditation. Each subsequent attempt culminated in the same result no matter how carefully I checked each piece of entered information. This process of action and repetition felt particularly resonant with the political climate as an examination of the necessity for (and, often, futility of) persistence in the face of frustration and failure."

Susan Wheeler's (East Millstone, New Jersey) new *Assorted Poems* is a selection from her first four books of poetry; she is also the author of a novel, *Record Palace*. She teaches at Princeton University.

"I knew I wanted to use the president's voice and his immediate, specific experience, and that, given teaching commitments that day, I would have only the last hour of the day to write it. As for choosing the occasion, it struck me that journalists were making light of the queen's and the first lady's hug, but that it was a historically phenomenal event: the last blow to the Divine Right of Kings, one of the monarchy's foundational walls."

Dara Wier's (Amherst, Massachusetts) *Selected Poems* will be coming out from in fall 2009. She directs the MFA Program for Poets and Writers at the University of Massachusetts–Amherst. Awards include the *American Poetry Review*'s Jerome Shestack Prize and fellowships from the Guggenheim Foundation and National Endowment for the Arts. Recent books include *Remnants of Hannah* and *Reverse Rapture*, which was awarded the Poetry Center & American Poetry Archives 2006 Book of the Year Prize. She edits, with Emily Pettit and Guy Pettit, Factory Hollow Press.

"With poetry at my back, I sat and thought. One thought led to the next thought, with music and words providing conveyance, with the assignment in sight, until, as these things happen, the picture of that hopeful man passing his hand through the sky stirred up another thought and there it appeared I should stop. Poetry is a kind of superstition, or a casting of spells and a promise. There's a wake following every poem's appearance. Thanks to the project for asking me to think about days accumulating."

Joshua Marie Wilkinson (Chicago, Illinois) was born and raised in Seattle. He is the author of four collections of poems, most recently *The Book of Whispering in the Projection Booth*, and coeditor, with Christina Mengert, of a new anthology of poetry, conversations, and poetics called *12 x 12*. He was in Grant Park on election night.

"When I wrote this piece, Obama had only been president for about a month, and there were a number of articles being written about his difficult transition into vacuumed isolation: a potentially hazardous insularity from goings on into which the previous president receded deeply. Bored with arch 'poetic' approaches (whether inaugural in tone, stately in locution, or grave in admonishment), I figured I'd write mine in the mode of the poems for my friends I'd been doing over the last couple of years—trusting Obama'd be smart enough to roll with the references but assuming, too, that the assistants sussing the blog might need some cues to get it onto his screen for eleven seconds or so."

Rebecca Wolff (Athens, New York) is the author of three books, *Manderley*, and *Figment*, and *The King*. She is the founding editor of *Fence* magazine and Fence Books.

"I wrote this poem for/about the presidency very very quickly on the morning of my day, out of spontaneous emotion and varieties of experience, not to mention hope and belief and fear. I tried not to let my fear overwhelm my hope and belief (jug ears vs. assassination)."

Matthew Zapruder (San Francisco, California) is the author of two collections of poetry, *American Linden* and *The Pajamaist*. His collaborative book with painter Chris Uphues, *For You in Full Bloom*, will be published in 2009, and his third book of poems, *Come On All You Ghosts*, is forthcoming in 2010. He is an editor for Wave Books.

"In this poem, I am first thinking about the Phoenix Mars Lander, which sent its final transmissions and then fell silent during the same week Obama was elected. This poem comes from the part of me that fears for the fate of everything, including the words 'hope' and 'change,' which sometimes seem so insignificant and meaningless in the face of the challenges that are before us."

Rachel Zucker (New York, New York) is the author of four books of poetry, including *Museum of Accidents* and *The Bad Wife Handbook*, and is coeditor, with Arielle Greenberg, of *Women Poets on Mentorship: Efforts and Affections*. Zucker has three sons, teaches poetry, is a certified labor doula, and is studying to become a childbirth educator.

"Shocked and saddened by the news that my son's teacher has leukemia,

I started to think about 'change'—how it is good and bad, completely inevitable. The presidency was still very new then and despite the bitter weather and each individual's daily frustrations, I noticed an unmistakable warmth, openness, and camaraderie among strangers on the street. I felt a new intimacy with New Yorkers and with President Obama, whom I imagined—as I'd never imagined of a president—might actually care about my life. I wanted to describe this intimacy and the social and physical contact I have every day with the people of New York City."

ACKNOWLEDGMENTS

Thank you to Josh Goren (publicity), Tom Shakow (political consultation), Dan Shiffman (technical support), Lindsey Wallace (editorial and administrative assistance), and the English Department at Columbia College Chicago.

Elizabeth Alexander's process note is drawn from an interview published in the *Baltimore Sun*, January 30, 2009.

Index